The Problems With Men

By

Bobby Black

The Problems With Men

By

Bobby Black

Published By **OMG BOOKS**

Copyright © 2021 **OMG BOOKS**

All rights reserved

ISBN-13: 978-0-9934801-1-9

ISBN-10: 0993480119

Bobby Black Books

The Problems With Women (2015)

The Problems With Men (2021)

Bobby Black

Dedication

This book is dedicated to all the women who are tired of stale, lame men who have unfortunately had the marvellous privilege of encountering, tolerating and sometimes nearly killing the worst half of the human race - men.

It is also dedicated to the men who take the plunge. All those looking into themselves and trying to improve despite the struggles of life.

Contents

Acknowledgments	i
Introduction	1
Double Standards	5
The Ideal Man	13
Body Mass	34
Dress Up	39
Speak Up	42
Hard Of Hearing	47
Man Up & The Undesirables	52
Boys To Men	60
Mummy's Boy	69
Big Baby	73
Man Flu	77
One Trick Pony	80
Bromance	83
Men & Things	88

Mr Money	92
Broke Bums	96
Online Dating	102
Non-committed	110
Sperm Donors	114
Bastard	121
Control Freaks	124
Mr Abusive	128
Perverts	140
Sex	144
No Means No!	175
Mr Wrong	183
What Women Really Want	187

The Problems With Men

Acknowledgements

I must acknowledge my mother who over the years has shown me immense love and support, regardless of my imperfections. She is the greatest woman I have encountered.

I am also eternally grateful to my copy editor D.A.J.C. who has been a great help and has also contributed by sharing some of her own experiences which have helped shape this book.

I am extremely appreciative of my illustrator Natalie Evans who painstakingly dedicated her time to create the artwork for the cover in such short notice.

Thanks to all the women that I have spoken to who imparted with their own personal experiences, adding weight to my own viewpoint. Without them, this book would not be as detailed and complete as it is.

Introduction

Before going any further, I must say that I am a man and I suffer from many of the flaws mentioned in this book. It may seem that I am excluding myself from the shortfalls of these 'men' in the book. I am not. I am far from perfect, like all living creatures on this earth.

This book is about the problems with men, primarily the problems that affect our better halves, the princesses and queens - women.

Many women are looking for a good man. The truth be told a lot of women are struggling to find a good man. The search may take them years, sometimes decades and some women never seem to stumble upon a good man.

Many women are unhappy in their relationships. Finding the right guy can be a torturous quest. Prince Charming can remain a mythical character only written about in fairy-tales or shown in fictional romantic films. Or unfortunately he exists but for whatever reason he is unavailable or uninterested.

The quest that women go through is laden with emotionally unavailable men. From narcissists to fiercely shy introverts. Some that are aggressive and some of them violent. Men that are not empathetic, oblivious to the needs and wants of women. Men that have yet to grow up and mature into a fine specimen that know how to treat a lady. Their expedition is filled with men that have erectile dysfunction or men that are only interested in sex.

Women suffer in their experiences with these men every day.

This book is about that suffering.

This book is about the problems with men.

I know what you are thinking. I myself am a man, what gives me the right to represent women, to talk about the problems they encounter with men? As one woman who read my previous book asked me recently, "What do you know?"

Well for starters, I am an empathetic person who understands the plights women grapple with the troubled men they come across. I have listened to my partners, female family members and friends. Women talk a lot and speak of all the dramas and dilemmas they face and have faced in their interactions with men. If you pay attention and listen then you will understand them a lot more.

I have been in quite a few relationships with women who have agonised about their past lovers, boyfriends and husbands. They have told me about their experiences, confiding in me even after we have broken up.

They have also expressed their numerous disappointments in me, telling me where I have gone wrong and where I have gone right. They have shared their hopes and dreams and described their ideal man.

In writing this book I have spoken to women to verify my insights but I also spoke to women to listen and understand their points of view on the masculine sex. Many of those points are mentioned in the book and are spoken in their voice with a hint of the Bobby Black sarcasm and humour.

Plus, I am an advocate of free speech. I am free to express my views and opinions until the politically correct police and the thought police destroy the voices and minds of the opinionated and the free thinkers.

Additionally, as I mentioned before, I wrote a book called The Problems With Women so it is only fair that I balance it out as we are both equal - different but equal - so we both will face a hammering for our faults that annoy and frustrate the opposite sex. I recognise the faults in both sexes from reverse viewpoints.

This book gives insights into how and what women think about men. This book does not border on the side of ambiguity. It tells it straight about what women really think about men.

It will inform men about how to approach and treat women. It may improve how some men deal with women if they pay attention to what this book is screaming at them.

This book will also open the eyes of some women who are yet to find out the pitfalls of men. It may help them avoid being in unhappy, emotionally abusive and or violent relationships.

It is written in a humorous way as to keep all entertained but there is many a truth told in jest. Parts of this book may be hard to swallow for some men - think about what women have to go through, and if the cap fits...

Happy reading.

Bobby Black

Double Standards

I know in the introduction I said men and women are different but equal but let us be fair, that is bullshit. In theory women are - but in reality, they are not treated equally at all. The problem with men is that they are full of double standards. Men are self-centred creatures that want to have their cake and eat it.

Apparently, it is cool for a man to sleep with as many women that are willing to, but if a woman takes the same approach to life she is labelled with all sorts of derogatory names.

Why is it that a woman cannot explore her sexual desires with as many men as she pleases?

The more experience anybody has in the sexual arena, the more chances they will get to hone their skills and satisfy themselves and others in future sexual encounters. Keep in mind the 10,000-hour rule: where spending 10,000 hours doing something will make anybody a master at that skill.

Men stare at porn all day. Dreaming of sleeping with one of those porn stars and then turn around and call a female friend or family member a slut for sleeping around. A woman does not even necessarily need to sleep with many men for her to gain the unwanted attention from people who consider her actions shameful.

The problem here exists not with women but with men and their overinflated egos. They cannot bare to think that a woman that they love has been with many men, or any men in many cases.

Their subconscious insecurities lead them to wonder where they lie in the mind of the woman. Men are competitive, they want to be the best. They want to be the man she most desires. They want to be the best sexual partner ever. Rather than face up to the possibility that they may not be the best, they would rather eliminate the competition and go for a woman that has only a few, or better still, no previous sexual partners. That way they can only be the best. Or, at least have a much higher chance of being the best.

When they come across women that do not fit this ideal, they label them with offensive names rather than accept that they are human too and have desires just as men do.

To be fair, women can be their own worst enemy in this case as many women will call their fellow women nasty names and pass snide remarks.

Last time I checked, at the time of writing, it's 2021, not centuries earlier. The days of witches being tied up and stoned are over. Grow up and live and let live.

Sticking to equality, check out how much men and women get paid for doing exactly the same jobs. Why do women get paid less for doing the same jobs? Do they deserve less pay for doing the same things? Men simply do not possess the intelligence to recognise the value in treating women equally.

Let us not beat around the bush - men are sexist, whether that be consciously or unconsciously.

I personally believe we all have an inkling to understand and relate to ourselves and those similar to ourselves before we relate to others. That produces a natural biasness which inherently hinders others who are dissimilar from us.

That is no excuse for men to think it is one rule for them and another for women.

Even though in most modern western societies, the Law gives the appearance of equality, in reality it is a myth - the equality myth.

Things are changing. Laws and attitudes are evolving in different environments, albeit at different speeds across the globe. In Saudi Arabia they recently changed the law to allow women to drive and to travel abroad without the permission of a man, which they were forbidden from doing up until then.

The #MeToo movement has also highlighted a lot of sexual harassment inside and outside of the workplace, that women have had to endure for decades, if not centuries.

Often women are viewed by men as nothing more than sexual beings for men to perv over and exploit, or bimbos that do not know or understand anything slightly complex or important.

A recent study in the US revealed that you are likely to live longer if you have a heart condition if your doctor is female. If your doctor is male, but he is surrounded by female colleagues, your life expectancy is also improved, although not by as much as it would be if your doctor is female.

Women are not just pretty faces. They are people who can contribute just as much as a man. In some cases, more than their male counterparts.

Another problem with men which is definitely a double standard is that men on the whole are as messy as can be - if we are being honest, they are dirty bastards. There could be cups gathering mould on the floor of their bedroom, with dirty and clean clothes strewn all over the place. Dirty plates in the bed underneath the covers. Basically - looking like somebody burgled his house and forgot to clean up. He would not even notice and get up and get on with his day, day in, day out.

All of a sudden, this lazy slob miraculously finds himself a girlfriend who, when she comes over to his, tidies up and makes it look like she hired cleaners to clean his messy environment to look like a showroom for new build apartments.

They fall in love and end up living together. He is still a disaster waiting to happen when it comes to being clean and tidy. But yet when he sees mess - sometimes mess that he created - he now has a go at his lovely girlfriend that turned his jungle of a habitat around.

That, my dear friends is the problem with men.

Picture this: A woman is in a relationship and has a child with her partner. Unfortunately, that relationship did not work out and they break up. She is left with custody of the child and the father has visiting rights. She does everything that a parent should do for her child. In many of society's eyes she is frowned upon as a single mother.

The father is seen pushing the pram down the street on the weekend, and he is championed for being a good dad - even though it is his job. The same job that the mother does 12 days in a row until he picks up the child on the Friday and drops the child back on the Sunday.

If a woman has to take time off to deal with an issue associated with her child, it is a problem. She gets the death stare and the reluctant blessing of the time off - if she is lucky. If not, she would have to fight for that time off or rearrange her work schedule with a colleague that is willing to cover or swap shifts depending on the nature of the job.

If a man does the same, he is praised for being such a wonderful father.

I am not even sure if that is a problem with men or society in general...

Keeping on the subject of what society deems as acceptable and unacceptable, if a man dates a younger woman on the whole people are okay with that, some people might frown upon it. But across the board it seems to be tolerated at the least. It has been happening for a long time so that might have something to do with it.

If on the other hand a woman decides to date a younger man, she could be looked down upon like a witch in medieval times. Family members and so-called friends will chat behind her back and in her face and not in a positive manner. One rule for men, another rule for women.

A man will ask a woman how she feels or what is going on in her mind. He is trying to gauge how she is feeling, what type of mood she is in, to see how he should treat her or whether he can help or support her.

Lovely man.

The problem with these inarticulate men is that if the woman asks him what is going on, his mind will go blank. He will fail to muster any meaningful words. He may go silent or just say he is fine. He might tell her to leave him alone. His brain cannot handle such confusing questions. She is only trying to be helpful, understanding and supportive but he cannot answer the question to save his life.

The list of things where women are not looked upon as equal to men is as long as a piece of string that could wrap around the earth 10 times over. Saying anything different is a lie and a falsehood.

It is fair to say that women do benefit in some areas over men. Many nightclubs are cheaper for women, or even free. They also are more likely to be let into the club than a man and are more likely to gain entrance before men amongst other things.

But overall men get the better side of the deal.

Let's be honest about it.

The Ideal Man

Many women are looking for the same or similar things in men. The list is romantically and painfully long because it is the small details that matter to women. Women can also be demanding in their expectations of men.

Although the list is quite extensive, I do not think most women realistically expect to find a man with all these qualities. Also, not every woman is looking for the exact qualities listed here. She may be looking for some and not for others.

Most women want a man that is handsome in their eyes. Remember beauty is in the eye of the beholder. What one woman finds attractive in a man's features may not be the same for another. One woman's lustful desire is another woman's absolute turn off!

What I would say though is that women want something decent to look at. So, if you look repulsive, sorry but that is your bad luck.

Some women prefer chiselled masculine features whereas others prefer an innocent looking baby face. Some women like clean shaven whereas the recent trend of beards in the last decade or so has seen a rise in their admirers.

The same could be said for hair. Some women like men with short hair whilst others are attracted to men with long hair and others like their men bald. This is all down to personal preference. No one man's physical appearance is going to be every woman's ideal fantasy. Having said that, there are some general traits that you will hear a lot of women express their desire for.

You often hear tall, dark and handsome floated about. Tall and dark can be easily verified however the handsome element is definitely down to personal taste.

If you are perceptive you will discover that women admire a man with nice eyes, whatever that means to them. I have heard that many times over the years. Nice eyes that look at you, seize your attention and pierce deep into your soul.

Nice teeth - a set of clean straight gnashers will do a lot to attract a female counterpart. Maybe part of that is to do with a man and his smile. Women tend to distance themselves from men with a grim looking face. Looking too serious and menacing most probably will not do you too many favours in the woman department.

Do not get me wrong, those type of men may have their following but it is more likely to be smaller in comparison to a man who has a nice friendly smile and seems happy the majority of the time.

People in general like happy people. It is endearing and it is contagious. Everybody wants to be happy or at least they say they do. In reality, they may or may not be doing much to get into that state but the thought is in the mind somewhere.

For that reason, we tend to like to be around happy people. It makes us feel good inside. That goes for men and women alike. Nobody likes to come home to a miserable partner. That is contagious too and nobody wants to catch miserableness.

A lot of women love a man with a muscular physique - not all but many. Men with broad shoulders that make a woman feel that; if she is with him, she will be protected. Look how many women drool over celebrities with their 6 and 8 packs. In comparison, there is not a great amount of demand for male celebrities to show off their Father Christmas beer bellies.

I am sure there are a few women that want to hold onto a well-rounded man like a teddy bear, but in general it is not considered attractive. For example, some say they prefer a man that is not in shape because it makes them feel less conscious about their own flaws.

Having said that, when women pay to see male strippers, they like to see a nice muscular body. They are not paying to see someone who looks obese or anorexic.

If one of those fits your body type, I am sorry to offend you but it is true. Either of those body types are not good for your health or for your self-confidence. If you are reading this and thinking; "that sounds like me", then you should go and do some exercise.

Everyone could do with some exercise.

For starters, it is good for your physical health. You will decrease the chances of you suffering from many illnesses and diseases. That includes cardiovascular exercise as well as muscular exercise. Do some research and find some work outs that work for you or if you need to be guided or encouraged, find a gym partner or a personal trainer. You will be doing yourself a favour!

Exercise is also good for your mind.

Endorphins are a form of feel-good chemicals which are released when you do things like exercise or have sex.

So, go and do some exercise and get yourself into shape. Eat healthy and feel good about yourself. Do not complain about me being insensitive to your feelings. See it more as a kick up the bum. Sometimes you have to be cruel to be kind.

You hear women talking about guy's bums. They like guys with big, firm bums. I have not noticed men rushing out to buy big bum implants just yet, you never know what the future holds, but I have been hearing women saying stuff like "Ooo look at his bum" or "He has got a nice big bum" since I was a child.

I have also detected that women like a man with strong, toned legs. I have read on many online dating profiles of women stating things such as "If you have got skinny chicken legs do not bother contacting me!"

Yes - I have tried online dating over the years to many mixed results. The thing with online dating is that you can get inundated with information about women and what they want. They do not all write a full biography with a list of criteria - but many of them do.

They write their likes and dislikes and their preferences.

One thing that stands out is that women are not too keen on the vertically challenged. No disrespect to midgets intended, but the vast majority of women are not interested in a man that is shorter than them with or without heels.

In fact, they tend to prefer a man that is not the same height as them when they are in heels. They want a man that is taller than them. It may seem strange but even many women that are short, let's say 4"11, would like a man that is 6" or over.

And the world wonders why so many guys suffer from short-man syndrome.

It is no good if you have got the looks but you dress like shit. A woman wants a man that dresses well in her eyes. Each woman's eyes may differ in what their sense of fashion and style is. For instance, some may like the rough and rugged look whilst others may favour a smart and suave look, this all depends on the female and her individual tastes.

A lot can be said about what men look like but on the whole many women are not totally stuck up on what a guy looks like. It is true that the younger generation in general are a lot more aesthetic about things than the generations before them.

Everything is Photoshopped or filtered to look more or less perfect nowadays. So, they are sold a dream of everything looking great. When in reality not everything is as stunning as the mind can imagine.

Back in the days before Photoshop existed things did not look perfect. Everything had flaws that you could see but it did not matter. Those generations were brought up to accept what they were given with all their flaws and imperfections.

Older people tend to realise it is not exactly what is on the outside that counts as much as what is on the inside. Life generally teaches you that.

Younger people in general tend to be more superficial. It is all about what it looks like to them. Even the older generation were young once and carried a similar mind-set to a degree, even if they do not want to admit it. What really matters to women is what a man's character is like. How does he treat them? How does he make her feel? Does he make her stomach feel funny inside? I do not mean does he make them feel like they are going to vomit either.

Is his conversation exhilarating? Does he keep her mind ticking? How does he carry himself and does he impress her?

These are just a few things that attract women whether that be consciously or subconsciously. People do not always know why they are attracted to things and people, but it does not stop the attraction. The subconscious mind works in mysterious ways.

Nearly every woman on the planet will tell you that they love a man that can make them laugh. A man that can make a woman laugh until her belly hurts, can actually laugh his way into her bed. When we laugh, we smile, when we smile, we feel happy and good inside.

These are the feelings that everybody craves. If your jokes are as funny as a funeral service, or worse still you have not got a sense of humour, forget about it. Go home and wank for the rest of your life!

Do not get me wrong, women like a man that is serious when he needs to be. If you are always joking especially when it is not the right time, you will piss her right off. Be serious when you need to be but do not take yourself too seriously.

Winning a woman's heart may be considered a hard thing to do but keeping a woman's heart after a man has won it can also be a difficult achievement.

Especially since in the beginning of most relationships people tend to try to impress the other. That is when a man usually wins a woman's heart. Of course, no one can be expected to sustain the affection shown in the honeymoon period. Whilst there, nothing else seems to matter, you are in a bubble. But when reality sets in, you realise that you have other responsibilities; bills to pay, work to do and it would be too exhausting to match that same level of enthusiasm. Having said all that, you cannot fall too far below the initial treatment.

This is a reason why women will give you less, why she may cheat, why she may leave you. Because you are not the man you used to be.

Heard that one before?

I am sure you have, along with; "you have changed" or "remember how you used to be so;" followed by a long list of positive adjectives. Literally telling you that you are not good enough anymore.

What she may not mention is she has had plenty of offers from many other guys, be it at work or place of study, on social media or just in public, like on the commute to work; the guy that was eying her up for years found the courage to strike up a conversation and they chat all the time now and he is showing the same if not more enthusiasm than you were in the beginning, let alone now. She has resisted up until now but if she does not see an improvement, who knows...

Because she may no longer feel as connected to you as she used to. Women need conversation. They like someone who can stimulate their minds. Win their minds and their bodies follow. Satisfy their bodies alongside their minds and their heart is yours.

But you have to keep it up, pun intended. Not just your penis but your efforts. There is only so long that your efforts in the beginning will count for. A woman might stay with you and may never cheat even if you put in less effort as time passes.

But she will be unhappy.

You might think, so what?

Well guess what? If she is unhappy, she will make your life a misery.

She will moan at you until you do not even feel like going home after work. She is not moaning because she enjoys moaning (unless of course she does love moaning) she is moaning because she is unhappy and frustrated.

She will give you less and less sex unless she really loves and/or needs it. But a woman's libido is usually based on her mood and happiness. If she is unhappy, she is less likely to be in the mood for sex. Especially if you are the root of her unhappiness. When she is happy and she feels connected to you, she will be much more likely to have sex with you. In fact, she will be making love.

Putting her all into it.

Sometimes women have sex because of their hormones. They do not always realise it, but sometimes they just feel horny and they want sex. That may or may not have anything to do with you, but sometimes it is just because their hormones are acting up. I believe it is her body's way of telling her that she is ready to conceive or it may just be that she needs to relieve some stress.

Men's minds are not that complex. When a man meets a woman, he is thinking about how hot she looks and his mind is likely to wander over to thinking about having sex or wanting to have sex with this woman if he is attracted to her. If he is not attracted to her his mind will be blank like Homer Simpson's.

When a woman meets a man, her mind is ticking over like a supercomputer whether that is consciously or subconsciously. She is figuring out what she likes and dislikes about him. She is instantly debating whether you are interesting to her or not.

If a woman remotely likes you, she may ask simple questions that might seem innocent but really, she is summing you up. Do you tick the boxes of her criteria?

For instance, she may ask you your age. This is her summing up whether you fit into the age brackets she has set for herself. If your answer makes you too young or too old in her opinion; consider your application denied. You may be able to charm her and if she really likes you or wants something from you (like money) then you will become the exception to her rule, otherwise forget about it.

A man that is full of charm will attract women by the boatload. A man that knows how to communicate well with a woman will be well ahead of the competition. Charm and charisma go a long way. They give women a sense of spark and excitement. Women do not tend to get excited when they meet dull, boring men.

Women love a man that can read her without her even verbally telling him anything. It is called being attentive. Any of you guys heard of that? Most women do it all the time. Pay attention to your woman and you can find out so much about her. Not just her, but women in general as they tend to have many similarities.

Communication is not only the key to attracting women - it is the key to keeping them. You would never believe the number of women that complain about the lack of communication with their man. If you are not communicating with your woman, another man will.

It is all part of making a woman feel safe and secure. How many times have you heard that a woman wants a man that can understand her?

Millions, but you do not even realise because you fail to listen. She wants a man that listens to her and understands how she feels and the way she thinks.

She does not want to feel like she is talking to a wall. She wants a man that responds, not talk over her, but a man that can articulate himself well and prove that he has heard what she said by making relevant responses.

Society puts a lot of pressure on women to look perfect and behave perfect, whatever that is. This leads to many women always questioning themselves. What many women are looking for in a man is reassurance. A little bit of reassurance can give them a great boost of confidence and a lack of it can make them question themselves even more. The more positives a woman gets from you the better she will feel about herself. The happier she will be around you.

This is not to say women need a man's approval for anything. If a woman is in a relationship then having reassurance from the person that is important to them, their man, is only going to be beneficial to both parties.

Consider the opposite. A man always putting a woman down. How do you think that will affect her confidence and self-esteem?

Most women love to be complimented, genuinely complimented - not falsehoods as sooner or later they will realise you are talking drivel. They do not want to be over complimented as that may come across as baloney.

For instance, a woman gets her hair or her nails done, she would like to think that you have noticed and that you like it. They want a man that can make them feel good about themselves. This is not to say that they need a man for this, they would just like these traits in a partner rather than having a man that belittles them all the time or pays little interest in them.

Part of identifying whether a man is fit to be part of her life will include his level of intelligence. A woman needs to know that a man is smart enough to give her good advice and wise enough to guide any children that poke their way into their relationship if they are not already in existence. They will want to know that this man will make good decisions for their future.

Of course, the level of a woman's intelligence counts here. She will only be able to judge your intelligence from her own level of intelligence. That means there is somebody for everyone. A woman with a high level of intelligence will judge more harshly than a woman with a lower level. So, if you are not the brightest spark in the box, no need to worry too much - there is still someone that will accept you for your shortcomings.

Women are studying you long before children come into the equation to see if you would be a good father. Are you reliable? Will you make enough income to help support the family? Do you have the types of attributes they want to see in their own children? These are a few of the questions that may pop up in a woman's mind while they spend time getting to know you.

Almost all women love a man with a warm heart and a kind spirit. At least they say they do and romanticise about it in their minds, but a lot of women do not end up with a man that fits this description. If you are a horrible, selfish git you might still get lucky.

Women know that they can be a handful sometimes. That is why they would prefer a guy that is patient and tolerant. A guy that can put up with her mood swings or better still, one that can help lift her mood when she is down. But at the same time, she does not want a doormat that she can walk all over. She wants a man with a backbone that can handle himself and handle her too. I do not mean physically abusing her either.

Wealth and money can attract a woman temporarily. The glamour and glitter can have the effect of getting a woman's attention and much more. But if that is all you have got going for you, then it will not last. Women like substance in the long run. Saying that, a lack of money will also encourage a woman to lose interest in you. Make something of yourself and prove you can play your part financially within a relationship.

There is no point in having money and being as tight as Russell Brand's skinny jeans. A poor man that is generous will attract a woman much more than a rich man that acts like Scrooge.

A woman likes to be pampered. She likes to be taken out. She wants gifts, she wants a man that will go shopping with her and not complain. A man that enjoys the experience and gives valuable feedback. So, if you are not into attending, do not get jealous of her gay best friend who will fit that role much better than you!

Many women like to be treated like ladies. They like a gentleman that opens the door for them and does things to make her feel special.

There is no point in being the perfect gentleman some of the time and then other times you are a complete twat. Women like consistency.

If you text a woman every morning then all of a sudden you do not text in the morning she is going to wonder why? Why has your pattern of behaviour changed? Then if you go back to texting her every morning, she is going to question what happened in those days that you did not text. Do not be surprised if she grills you about those absent days, you left a void that needs explaining - so explain.

When a woman opens up her heart and her legs to a man, she wants to feel respected. She has now made herself vulnerable, she does not want to be taken advantage of or be taken for granted. She wants to feel like she is being appreciated. Be grateful for the woman in your life or do not bother in the first place.

Most of all, a woman wants to feel loved. They want to feel cared for. They want to feel like they bring warmth to your heart like you bring warmth to theirs. Love is an extremely strong emotion. Love is the ultimate positive feeling that one can feel for another.

Throughout the animal kingdom many animals dance to impress their primates. Within the human race the same rules apply. Women like a good dancer, for starters if a man gets up and dances it shows he has confidence. If he can move his body well and in rhythm to the music it also implies to the mind, he is likely to be good in bed. A man dancing in sync with a woman can be a turn on for both parties, it is sensual and intimate.

But if you look like a buffoon or you cannot help stepping all over a woman's feet, then stay in your seat and do not embarrass yourself. As a good dancer is a turn on for a woman, a terrible dancer is a turn off. I do not know what possesses some men. If Drake's dancing makes you look bad then you seriously need to re-evaluate your life or get some dancing lessons.

Drake can get away with dancing terribly because he is Drake. You cannot!

It goes without saying if you are rubbish in bed you are going to struggle with most of the women you come across. You better read some books about what women like or just stick to porn and have imaginary women in your head.

If you cannot even get it up, stay at home, buy some Viagra or do not even bother chatting to women. Keep yourself in the friend zone. Women do not want to put up with a guy who cannot even get an erection. What is wrong with some defected men?

Another problem with men is that they are lazy fucks when it comes to housework. A woman loves a man that helps around at home and can cook. Too many men think cooking is something you do with the microwave.

A woman will love a man that brings out the best in them. A man that helps her feel good about her life. One that helps her feel good about herself. A man that she respects and looks up to. If she does not respect you then you need to look into yourself and ponder why? The problem with men is they do not even think about these things until it is too late. If your woman is not feeling great then after a while, she will treat you like a prick, look elsewhere or leave. Or worse - she will do all three.

Some of you reading may be thinking to yourself that a lot of this spiel might sound like common sense. What I have come to realise is common sense is not that common. It is actually quite rare; just because you know it, do not assume that everyone else does because many people do not! They should rename it rare sense.

It is true the criteria for most women's ideal man is extensive. A woman will usually have some expectation when she enters the relationship world but in reality, she does not have much to measure that by due to her lack of experience. This will lead to her being quite unrealistic in her expectations or open and flexible to whom they go into a relationship with.

After a relationship or two the flexible woman list starts to extend and become lengthier by the day, because of her likes and dislikes that she picks up from being in those relationships. This usually grows until she approaches the age of 30 and beyond.

If by this time she has not found a suitable man and she has yet to have children then her standards will eventually begin to drop as reality sets in and she realises that she was unrealistic in her expectations or that the ideal man she was searching for is in very short supply and she failed to attract or keep one so far.

Now with her fertility rate dropping on a daily basis, a panic will eventually settle in as her deadline looms. Her attitude is likely to become a lot more adaptable to accommodate her want to have a child.

This is, if she does not have children and wants them. If she has one or some, or does not want children, her list could end up growing longer and longer, until she ends up like that meme of a skeleton with a handbag sitting on a bench still waiting for the perfect man.

Good luck with that.

Some women are still waiting, but others are fine being single forever. They would rather die alone than settle with a muppet as a partner. So, if you are cluttered with these problems, then you better adapt or accept your place as a skeleton on the bench too.

Body Mass

Women do not only observe what a man's face looks like they also have a good look at his body mass and hope to see bulging muscles and a six-pack loitering underneath a man's garments. Not all women, but many, if not most.

Some women will not even consider you if you are not in shape. That is their preference. They like brawny men, with broad shoulders, strong arms, a chest like two big pillows, and strong, firm legs. Anything else is a no to them.

Yet the problem with some of these muscular dudes is that that is all they are; a great big lump of chiselled body mass. Seriously lacking in any intelligence, personality and charisma.

Women will get all excited about how the way this guy looks. Staring at his muscles protruding through his clothing and their heart starts to pound in their chest as they get goose bumps looking at his physique.

Then they start to talk. Sooner or later her enthusiasm starts to dwindle away as she realises that the conversation is dead. He has nothing interesting to say. He does not even seem that interested in her. There does not seem to be any intellect there. His humour is not funny and all he talks about is exercise, muscles and his diet.

Not much more to him than that.

That is great if she is a gym freak too. If not, she will be bored to death and wondering how they started talking in the first place and how to shut him up.

Many of these gym freaks are narcissists; they are only interested in themselves. All they care about is their physique and what they look like in the mirror. They actually look in the mirror more than women.

No woman wants to be competing with a man for mirror time!

They are forever in the gym and when they are not, they are working out at home or tensing their muscles in the mirror every 5 seconds. They have little time to focus on a woman. They are nice to look at but awful to be around. Full of themselves with little to offer women other than a good view.

Some of these guys have personality disorders because they did not naturally get to that size. They used steroids. They are snappy and get agitated quickly.

They are actually quite scary because they have ferocious tempers and can fly off of the handle at any moment. They have split personalities. You do not know if and when you are talking to them or the drugs.

Women fall in love with Bruce Banner and then later on they realise that he is the Hulk.

Then there is the guy who forgot to take care of his body at all. Overeating, overweight pile of mess. His belly is so big that he looks like he is about to give birth anytime soon.

Women dread having sex with these guys. They are very particular about what sexual position they are going to have sex in if they do indulge. If missionary is your favourite position forget about it. Which woman do you know that wants to be flattened during a time when she is supposed to be receiving pleasure?

They want to have fun not be squashed to death!

It also shows a lot about a man's attitude. You might just come across as a lazy, cannot be bothered type of person. She does not want a man that is only interested in himself but neither does she want a man that does not make an effort.

If he looks as if he cannot see his fully erect willy when he looks down, then she might run a mile when he approaches her.

No need to worry, he will be too slow to catch up.

That is no reason for you to give up though.

Take a leaf out of the ugly man's book (see Man Up & The Undesirables) and work on your character. There is nothing wrong with being nice and developing some charisma.

Women might also worry about how much it takes to feed you. She will be secretly thinking to herself he better know how to cook and actually make use of that knowledge. Many people can cook but will not, but he cannot be expecting her to be cooking like she has got to feed the 5000 but all at once with one person.

As mentioned before, some women do not mind a guy that is a little bit overweight. It makes them feel less self-conscious about their own weight. Not many women prefer a man that is much slimmer than them though. You will make them feel like they have to lose weight to keep up with you.

Women like to feel protected. They do not want to be walking down the street with a man that is just a bag of bones. Having a man of a decent size is like having pepper spray in your purse. You may never even have to use it but it is there all the same just in case, helping you feel safe.

It is all that more reassuring.

She does not want to be with a beanpole that looks underfed and malnourished. She will be thinking about feeding you and stuffing you up like Hansel & Gretel.

Sex can be another problem area here as a man's bones - not his sexual tool but his actual bones - can be painful if it digs into her side whilst being intimate.

Also, she does not want to feel like she is hurting you. She wants to enjoy the experience not worry that she might snap you in two.

Eat up. Go to the gym, get fit. Most of all, be nice. Personality always goes a long way.

Dress Up

Some men just cannot dress.

They look like a terrible mess. It is as if no thought goes into what they wear. Most women feel embarrassed walking around with a guy like that. Unless they themselves are just as embarrassing to walk the street with. Or they are blind as a bat and do not notice how badly these men dress.

These men are totally oblivious to how awful their attire appears. It is not that they are proud of how they dress or that they dress like a vagabond, know it and are just not bothered. These guys are simply unaware of how bad their clothing looks on them.

Worse still, is that some guys actually believe they look like the bee's knees. They are really proud of the way that they cannot dress. Women stand there looking at them thinking; "how on earth did they put on their clothes and turn out so shoddy?" "What mirror were they looking into to make them think that they have any sense of style or class?"

There are other guys that decorate themselves just as inadequately, but these guys could not give a damn. They could not give two hoots about how they look and some of them are actually proud of that.

No shame.

Yes, we all should not be too materialistic but the truth of the matter is your image makes a statement and leaves an impression. If you dress like you are homeless, do not be surprised when the security guard starts following you around when you are in a shop. And do not be surprised if you cannot find a girlfriend either.

Women want something good to look at, something pleasing to the eye and they also want to feel proud of their man. If you look like you have not changed your clothes for a week or two, how do you expect to attract the opposite sex?

Some of these guys are lucky enough to get a girlfriend. Maybe they are good looking, got some charm, or most probably they have got a few quid from the money they saved on not buying decent - or hardly any - clothes.

But these guys will usually fail to hold onto any women they attract when they do not change their underpants for days at a time. These men spend less than 5 minutes getting ready including bathroom time and pronounce that they are finished.

Do they even know the meaning of clean?

No woman wants to wait hours for a man to get ready but they at least want a guy that washes himself and his clothes - oh and changes his clothes, not just continuing to wear the same dirty briefs and clothes for weeks on end. A woman likes a man that smells nice, not one that stinks of foul bodily odour.

They want to be turned on, not turned off!

If you look like a tramp and you smell like a tramp do not expect to attract women. If by some miracle you do get a woman, do not expect her to stay if that is how you carry yourself.

It is just plain nasty. No woman wants to be married to Mr Twit unless she is Mrs Twit!

Take a little pride in your appearance and your hygiene. Do not be like Pete Hegseth who proclaimed not to have washed his hands in 10 years. Do not go around spreading the lurgies or coronavirus!

Disgusting!

Speak Up

Have you ever noticed that some men do not speak enough? How on earth are you supposed to understand them when they do not say much?

These men do not talk about what is on their mind or how they feel. They are like a closed book with an empty cover - not even an insert at the back. Just a plain, closed book. Open it up and the pages are blank.

Nothing to go by.

Women are very smart human beings. They usually have good emotional intelligence compared to most men. But they are not mind readers.

Women talk a lot. They express themselves. It is not hard to understand them, if you listen.

Men on the other hand do not really have much to say. They do not express their feelings; they tend not to tell you what they are thinking about.

They have a habit of leaving what is on their mind, in their minds, but then they get annoyed when women do not understand them.

Erm, where is the logic in that? That does not make any sense at all. If you spoke up and expressed yourself, a woman would have less difficulty understanding you and your stupid ways. But otherwise, her one tool is her emotional intelligence, which can only be so accurate.

Men are like politicians - as a matter of fact, most politicians are men.

If you do the math you will find that the majority of politicians are not like Donald Trump. If you ask Donald Trump a question you are likely to get a straight answer. You might not like the answer - but you are likely to get one.

Ask most politicians a question and they will beat around the bush and give you some waffle that does not answer the question. Ask a lot of men and they will do the same thing.

They are supposed to be men, so man up!

But unfortunately, these set of wimps will not.

Worst thing is the question being asked might not be that serious. A woman might just be asking if you can come somewhere with them on such and such a date.

Yet men will come up with the most cryptic answer when a simple yes or no will suffice.

Why is that?

Maybe he might not know the answer but he will spit out some drivel to make himself look good - or more likely sound like an idiot.

Some men do not like to make promises they are not sure they can keep so they come up with noncommittal answers. They do not want to disappoint you and tell you no, especially when the answer may actually be no.

On the flipside they may not want to tell you yes and then later tell you no. A vague answer that neither commits or disappoints is more useful and diplomatic.

To a woman though, this is absolute agony. You cannot think of many other things that can frustrate a woman more. They will be pulling their hair out trying to prise a clear answer from you. They will literally want to scratch your eyes out.

Women like clarity.

Men do not always like to talk about things or emotions. They tend to like to deal with them themselves. Men like to mull things over in their minds and deal with things alone. Women enjoy discussing things with others and resolving things mutually. Even for the simplest request of information many men will like to mull over that in his mind and come to a conclusion, whereas women will discuss that and come to a conclusion jointly.

Keeping things in your own mind and not verbalising anything will only cause problems. Problems that would not exist if you spoke up and shared your thoughts with your woman.

Women can be impulsive but along my journey in life, I have noticed women like to plan ahead and they also like some form of routine. Not knowing clear answers does not help them in these areas at all.

If the question posed is related to what a man thinks, his opinion or how he feels about something, this diplomatic approach is just as infuriating. A woman is usually trying to understand you as a person in order for her to be a better partner towards you.

If he has been put on the spot he may tell you any old rubbish, which might not necessarily be true, just to shut you up.

If you only forward false or ambiguous information about yourself you will leave holes in her interpretation of you. Later on, down the line you will wonder why she does not get you.

Remember, if you are not part of the solution you are part of the problem!

Learn the art of communication. Women are attracted to men that know how to articulate themselves well.

A good communicator will capture their audience's attention. They use charm and charisma and do not just spit out words like Speak & Spell, sounding all monotonous and robotic. They will adjust their style according to who they are speaking to. They will also clarify their point or points so they are understood by the recipient.

Learn to express yourself. Say what is on your mind. Use examples that whoever you are addressing can relate to. Use hand signals and body language to help people to understand you more clearly.

Speak up!

Hard Of Hearing

Men do not listen.

It is a fact.

They may act like they listen, but in truth they do not. You can tell a man something for his own good repeatedly, loud and clear but he will not listen. He will want to do things his own way.

Even if it is the wrong way.

Men like to defy logic.

Men do not like being told what to do. So, he may even know that a woman is talking complete and utter sense and know that his way is impossible, but just to please his own ego, he will carry on doing things the wrong way.

Complete imbecile!

Then when it all goes wrong; a woman will be thinking to herself "I knew it" or "I told you so".

A man will then try to justify his actions and say he done it his way because blah blah blah. Admit it, you did it your way because you are hard of hearing, you do not like taking advice from a woman and you do not like being told what to do, period.

There is nothing else to it - but many men will not admit these things. In fact, most men will not even admit that they were wrong to themselves. They will blame it on luck or something else. Because that is just how men are; stubborn and ignorant.

Men are not only hard of hearing in that sense. Men do not listen. A woman will pour out her heart like Cardi B, only for a man to forget everything that she said a little while later.

An example is when a woman arranges a date with her man. She confirms the date and details with him. The week that it comes up she will be like;

> "Do you need me to do anything so that that day runs smoothly?"

and the guy will be like,

> "Huh, what are you talking about?"

She will say:

> "For our date on Thursday, we are going to such and such a place."

He will be like,

"I cannot, I am doing such and such with so and so.

She will be like,

"But I told you ages ago."

He will be adamant that she never. Unless you have recorded proof, he will swear blind that you never said a word to him.

Why? Because men do not listen.

They will look like they are listening. They will stare you straight in the face and respond as if it is all logged in their memory and they will be ready to do whatever when the time comes, but in reality, you are talking to an empty shell.

It only nods and responds as if it is listening, but it is just some hollow headed dimwit standing in front of you that cannot remember simple sentences, dates and times.

Because later on, when the time comes to recall whatever was spoken to him, he will swear blind that you are lying or you have suddenly developed Alzheimer's or you are imagining things like a 5-year-old with an imaginary friend, as if you are part of the Rugrats in their pretend playground.

Because there is no way that he never listened to you, because his mind works just like a supercomputer that does not suffer from any technological problems.

No way.

It cannot be his poor memory; it must be that you are delusional. The truth is men are hard of hearing and that is it! He probably will not admit it, but men do not listen.

A woman will ask a man nicely to do something. He will respond in his usual reactive way as if he has heard what she has said and is going to do as he has been told. When you go to check if what you requested to be done has been completed you will find out that it has not. As mad as you may be, you will hold your nerve and attempt at asking nicely again and get a similar cooperative response as before.

The problem with men is a lot of men do not understand nice. Some men only understand harsh and angry communication. They will complain about how worked up and angry you have become as you ask for the umpteenth time. But they are much more likely to do as you have asked of them.

The same may be true if you have asked him not to do something. He will say, "okay babe" and you will think he has got the message. You can talk as pleasantly as you please but the message only connects when it is sent with a coarse undertone.

Why? Because that is the only language that many men understand, anything else and they fail to take it seriously. They take you seriously when you are serious but then whinge about your seriousness.

Seriously?

Man Up & The Undesirables

Have you ever noticed it is always the guy that you are not interested in that approaches you?

A lot of the time the men that approach women are looking to sue their parents because of their ugliness. They have been given a serious disadvantage in life:

Their monstrous looks.

Yet no matter how unattractive their features some of these guys ignore all of that and still find the courage to approach the opposite sex. Many of them exude confidence when it comes to chatting up women and some of them are quite successful in their advances. What they lack in physical attractiveness they make up for with personality and charisma.

But what really makes some women shiver up and down their spines, is when that good-looking guy that catches their eye actually approaches them and oozes that charm and wit that gets them hanging off their seat and playing with their hair subconsciously because they have been both attracted and mesmerised at the same time.

Unfortunately, instead of the handsome prince they have been longing for, it is the ugly frog that comes up to them looking like some monster that has been scaring them in their sleep, giving them nightmares.

We all know beauty is in the eye of the beholder but if, in your eyes somebody is ugly, then in your reality they are ugly no matter what anybody else says.

Let's face it, some mothers can struggle to see some form of handsomeness in their sons when they are no longer children. Nearly every mother thinks their babies are beautiful. They may still be blinded by love whilst their sons are children and maybe even teenagers. But all of that dwindles once they have become men.

Horrid looking ones.

The sons that remind them of that drunken night when they slept with his dad, only to be shocked and horrified when they woke up in the morning to realise, they had sex with an ugly beast.

These guys look like they are wearing a Halloween mask, but they were just born that way. Their ugliness has taught many of them to be charismatic. Without it, they would be angry and life threatening like Little Z in the film City of God.

Ever wondered how that unattractive dude got that drop-dead gorgeous woman hanging off of his arm? His sureness of character got him far in life and many beautiful ladies along the way.

There is something about a man that has the confidence to come over and talk to a woman. On top of that, many women want to be chosen. If they choose you, they may be unsure as to whether you really like them, or they may also think that they may be the one that has to keep choosing things within the relationship.

A lot of women are dismayed when that dreadful looking guy looks their way and seems like he is about to approach. They see him coming and then avoid all eye contact, screaming in their minds "PLEASE DO NOT TALK TO ME!"

As he approaches, she pretends to be talking into the headphones connected to her phone forgetting that she is underground on a tube with no phone signal (this paragraph was written before 4g was available on the underground in London). He pounces and makes his move and she is internally panicking whilst trying to play it cool.

He speaks and she acts like she did not hear. But these ugly guys can be persistent. So, he gets closer and speaks louder. She is now having a panic attack in her mind and gives the minimal one-word answer praying that he goes away and leaves her alone.

"Hello, how are you?"

"Good."

"What is your name?" He asks.

"I have a boyfriend" she replies.

"That is a weird name" he says.

She then contemplates getting off of the tube at the wrong stop just to get away. Waiting to see if he is getting off at the next stop. He stays, she grabs her stuff and is gone.

The everyday turmoil of a woman.

But this is not to say that if you are an unattractive man that you automatically have the gift of the gab and have the greatest personality on the planet. Many have characters as ugly as their looks. And many attractive guys have equally charming and appalling personas.

There is that handsome guy that stares at you. You are attracted to him but this guy has not got the confidence to come and talk to you. You can sense something because he always looks in your direction with that longing look in his eye.

Sheepishly.

It may seem slightly exhilarating for a woman in the beginning, but if there is never any follow up then they will soon get fed up or annoyed with you looking their way every day.

You will either look like a stalker, or a wimp.

The problem with these shy guys is they do not have any balls. They may have testicles but before they approach a woman, they have already talked themselves out of it.

How? They are telling themselves; "she is so beautiful, she will never consider me." They question whether they are good enough and put her on a level way above their own paygrade.

They try to calculate a dialog in their brains, trying to figure out what they should say. Instead of going over and just starting some form of conversation, they have a by themselves meeting in their brain and fail to get around to talking to anybody but themselves.

They ask themselves, "what if she says no?" They build up all these anxieties that make their bellies turn over and then they walk away.

Empty-handed.

What if she does say no? Is your world going to crumble? If it does, then you need to man up and look at yourself.

These guys can easily become one of those 40-year-old virgins or a man that pays for sex, because they have not got any confidence when they are talking to women, and instead contribute to the sex trade.

Grow a pair of balls and stop being a victim.

A victim of your own fear!

Sometimes these guys stare at you blatantly and other times they look and look away as soon as they notice you have noticed them looking at you.

When a handsome prince finally plucks up the courage to come over and talk to you, he is a stuttering, mumbling disaster that lacks confidence and has not got anything interesting to say.

What a disappointment.

Guys, you need to realise that women want you to talk to them, they just want you to have some game. They want to feel like they are having a conversation that they never want to end, not feel like they are in a job interview or talking to a monotone repetitive robot.

Although, it is true that many women never allow a man to show off their sparkling personality because they reject them before even giving them a moment's notice. Being charismatic, and capturing her attention early on will provide you with an opportunity.

Some guys end up being as interesting as a plank of wood and then they wonder why all the ugly guys get all the girls. If the only thing interesting about you is your looks, you might actually get a girl or two but you will not be able to keep them, unless they are as dreary and as uninteresting as you.

Improve yourself as a person, find some hobbies and interests that are more than stroking your cock watching porn all day. Then at least you will have something to talk about and will not seem like a narcissistic prick that is only interested in the way he looks.

What many men will find out if they find the courage to talk to women, is that the vast majority of women are not going to stab you in the eye with their heel or spit in your face for approaching them.

They will find out that women are human, like us men. They will also find out that a woman telling them 'no' is not going to make them lose their house or their job. It hurts but it does not kill. It is like getting an injection at the doctors; the initial sting hurts a little but you will get over it. It is not the end of the world.

Instead of asking 21 questions try making natural conversation. Talk about the weather or current affairs. Talk about something relevant; If you are waiting for public transport, talk about the wait or how good or bad the transport is. Then let the conversation naturally flow. If the pandemic has not wiped us out, talk about coronavirus - but maintain social distancing (if still applies).

Compliment her on a piece of clothing she is wearing or tell her how nice her hair looks. Remember; most women loved to be complimented. The problem with most men is they fail to notice a woman's items of clothing or her handbag that may cost as much as his car. Because men are blind to these things. They fail to see the whole of a woman and only notice her boobs, bum or her pretty face and fail to detect anything else.

Detect them and compliment them and you may have better luck with women.

Or just carry on being an undesirable punk.

Boys To Men

What I have noticed is a lot of younger women tend to date guys around their own age. Why? Because it feels right. Mentally, dating someone older seems weird. Dating someone younger is a straight no-no!

The problem with guys their own age is that they are yet to mature. They are immature, egotistical idiots that have yet to understand much about the opposite sex. Their understanding of the realities of life itself is childlike, it is worse if they are still living at home with their families and have never tasted the reality of living in the real world where you have to pay for things and have actual responsibilities.

An older man on the other hand, has plenty of experience and will understand a woman and know how to treat them. But the fear is that they will use their knowledge and wisdom to take advantage of them. This can be true because some men are nothing but ruthless bastards. By all means not all, but a man of an older age is more likely to be mature in his ways and less likely to act like a prick.

The problem with older guys is that they have lived their lives. They can be boring with no sense of adventure. They would rather sit at home like some couch potato and have a heart attack if you suggest going out for a night out on the town. Unless they are going through a midlife crisis and suddenly want to challenge themselves. They act as if they just stumbled upon the fountain of youth and look like a complete idiot, grey haired and balding old man dressed in skinny jeans with jewellery to match.

Mutton dressed as lamb.

A younger man on the other hand, is full of life. They are more likely to enjoy life and do things off the cuff. They are young and they just want to have fun and they do not look out of place having it!

Older women usually either want to settle down with a man their age or older. In some circumstances they just want to enjoy themselves and have fun, a lot of the time because they are recently divorced or have split up from a long-term relationship, in that case they may seek a younger man.

Why? Because it makes them feel young again and also the sex can be exhilarating. They will not be tied down to an old fuddy-duddy who wants to grow even older with them. They want a breath of fresh air; they want some excitement.

Young guys are full of energy, are less likely to take life too seriously and sexually, can go over and over again. Whereas an older man might go once or twice and that is him done.

That is if he can keep it up at all.

The problem with younger guys is that they are all about sex.

There might not be much more to them. That may be all they want you for. An older man is more likely to be interested in you as a person. He will appreciate you and actually indulge in getting to know your character not just the physical form of your body. You can have decent conversations and enjoy each other's company.

The problem with older men is they think they know everything. You cannot tell them anything. They know everything because they have lived for 1000 years already. This can also be a problem with men in general, but younger men will know they are out of depth if they encounter conversations or situations they have never come across before. They may take a humbler stance because of this. Whereas, older men are stuck in their ways, they will believe they know all.

It is great that younger guys can be more unassuming in unfamiliar surroundings but the problem with younger men is that when it comes to sex, they might not know what they are doing. All they know about is penetration. They are likely to rush and know little about foreplay or after-play for that matter. They are likely to be selfish and only be interested in their own satisfaction. Totally oblivious of the needs of a woman and whether she has been sexually satisfied.

An older man will usually know about conversing and getting a woman's mind into the mood and emotionally satisfying her so she feels at ease before sex has even started. They are also more likely to take things slower. Kissing, hugging and caressing a woman. Knowing which buttons to press to get a woman's body ready for the ultimate act. Once commenced, they will know what they are doing and how to read a woman, making sure she enjoys the experience. He may hold her in his arms afterwards, instead of just rolling over and falling asleep such as a young guy is likely to do.

Let no lies be told, this can be a problem with men regardless of their age.

Another problem with older guys is that they look it. They look old and wrinkly; their hair turns grey and recedes - if they still have any left. Basically, their best years of looking youthful are behind them. They look like a grape that has turned into a raisin. In some cases - they look ready to be taken to a hospice.

Most younger guys do not have to worry about this. They look youthful, like the models in the pictures, the famous sports athletes and most of the other celebrities that are presented by the media that women drool over. Younger men look brand new. Fresh out of the box. They still have hair and do not need to worry about their hairline. Unless they are Wayne Rooney, who had a hair transplant at the tender age of 26. He has always looked old since he was in his teens, poor sod.

But the problem with younger guys is many of them do not know what they want. They are still finding themselves. They do not know exactly what to do with their lives or who to do it with. They may find the perfect girl only to disregard her because they want to experiment and be with different women. They are yet to understand the true value of things, or more specifically, women.

Whereas an older man is usually sure of himself, his wants and needs. He does not need a lifetime to decide whether a woman is right for him or not. You either are, or you are not, it is as simple as that.

The problem with older guys is they are nearly dead. Women on average tend to live longer than men so having an older guy means a woman is likely to lose the man she has chosen to be with way before she has even begun thinking about dying.

A younger man has a lot more years in him. If he is a woman's age or younger, she is likely to spend more time with him and less time grieving after his death.

But the problem with some of the younger men is that they are broke! They are yet to establish themselves financially. They cannot afford to take you anywhere nice or buy you any decent gifts. If they do, they are breaking the bank and they will be penniless until payday. When they do get any cash, they are footloose and fancy-free, wasting it on irrelevant goods that hold very little value.

If a younger guy does have a few quid he is likely to be the most obnoxious and arrogant person you will ever come across. His money will become a substitute for his character - or lack of it.

An older guy is more likely to be in a financially comfortable position and can afford to spoil you rotten without breaking the bank. He will probably be less full of himself and more modest.

When it comes to compatibility, I personally do not believe age should be a deciding factor, as age does not define somebody's level of maturity. Neither does it define whether someone will take advantage of another; that is usually defined by someone's character.

When it comes to deciding whether to be with someone based on their age there are things to consider. A man and a woman at the same age of 20 have spent the same amount of years on the planet, but women tend to be more mature for their age, which means that she may be the same age in numbers but a lot older in maturity. A man and a woman at the age of 30 are more likely to be similar in maturity, as a man is likely to catch up a little as his years progress.

What is more important, is whether you find this person interesting. When they talk, do you listen? Do the subjects they talk about interest you, or is this guy as exciting as watching paint dry?

Does he listen to you when you are speaking and offer sensible feedback, whether that be an understanding of what you have said or good advice that takes into consideration your points? Or, is he just a mind-numbing yes man that nods and mumbles back every now and again, or worse, does not even reply at all?

When you talk to each other does it feel like you have been talking for 10 minutes but in reality, you look at the timer on the call you have made, and a couple of hours have passed? Or is it whenever you talk, you are in a rush to finish the conversation because even the sound of his voice irritates your ears? Do you feel connected to this man?

Does he feel like your soul mate or just another ship passing in the night?

Do you like spending time with this man? Do you both enjoy the things you do together? Or are the things he does of no interest to you and leave you bored stiff wishing that you never met up with him and done something else?

Do you want to go out and party while he wants to stay at home and watch TV or vice versa? These things have no relevance to age and more to do with somebody's interests and personality.

Are you on the same wavelength? Are your goals to travel and have fun or are they to work as hard as possible, save up and purchase a property?

It does not matter what your goals are, it matters whether his goals, morals and principles match yours. If they do not match up, then you might as well throw him away like a used mask, as it is unlikely to work and you are better off putting your energy and efforts elsewhere.

There is something else to consider; if you are a young woman, you may not know yourself that well. You might not have experienced much in life as yet, even though in your mind you may believe you know all there is to know, and you might not have developed all of your interests. 5 years ago, something may have been very relevant and important to you but now, 5 years later it means little or nothing to you. This may continue for a few years ahead, as we are constantly changing and evolving, especially in our younger years. So, you may grow apart from whomever you choose to be with whether they are your age or whether there is an age gap.

If you do things together, experience similar things together, keep the communication flowing between you two, appreciate one and another and perceive your partner in a good light these are things that are likely to keep you close and growing together, rather than growing apart. Of course, you must make sure you choose a guy that reciprocates and is not just all wrapped up in himself like pass the parcel.

Mummy's Boy

You can usually tell when someone is still living at home with their parents and has never moved out. They do not seem to realise the value of things.

They use things intermittently without thinking of the cost because their bills are usually next to nothing, if anything at all. Bills do not come in their name, they do not tend to have a tenancy agreement (who has a tenancy agreement with their parents?) and if they come up short one month, it is unlikely that they will be getting evicted or taken to court.

These men will stay at their girlfriend's house, eat them out of house and home, use the water as if there is an endless supply and the earth is not running out of resources. They leave lights on, forget to turn off appliances and forget that all these things cost money.

They offer little in currency to help her pay for these bills as they are oblivious that they even exist. Meanwhile his girlfriend bears the brunt of it, paying all her bills which cost more when he decides to come over from his mother's house.

The problem with some men is that they are not men at all. They are mummy's boys afraid to leave the nest. Some of these babies have never moved out of their mother's home and they are well into their thirties.

When you move out of your parents' home you get a sense of independence. You become your own person. You learn about life. You have to figure out how to make your money last and hopefully grow. You realise that if you do not clean up after yourself, nobody else will. If you flat share or live with your girlfriend, you learn how to get along with others and live with people that are not your family.

If you do not live with anybody else, you have to get up by yourself. Maybe with the aid of an alarm, but nobody is forcing you to be responsible. You live by your own rules.

No matter how well she gets along with your parents, women, hate to be with a man that cannot do anything because mummy or daddy said so. They want a man not a boy. Who needs permission to stay out late or sleep at his girlfriend's house?

What are you, 5?

Some men are totally under the control of one or both of their parents, regardless of whether they live at home or not. They do not make any decisions without mummies say so. Then they have the audacity to tell their woman what to do, when they cannot make decisions for themselves. Yet they now feel they can make decisions for you.

What a fucking cheek!

When two people enter a relationship, it is a dual partnership. That is why they say two's company and three's a crowd. That should mean that it is an exclusive relationship between the two of you. You have each other's back and you put each other first. Well, at least that how it should go.

The problem with men is some cannot help but bring their mothers into their relationship. It is as if the umbilical cord was never cut. Instead of feeling like his number one and only girl, you feel like you are constantly having to facilitate his mother. Worse is when a man always puts his mum first and you are just some afterthought.

At first it seems cute and respectful that he has so much time for his mum. After a while, you have to wonder if some incest is going on between them. Why does his mother's opinion always overrule yours? He almost treats her as if she is spreading her legs for him at night-time and as if you are not.

No woman wants a mummy's boy!

Women also feel uncomfortable walking from the bathroom to your bedroom in a towel with your family lurking, ready to catch glimpses of her travelling to and fro. Especially if you have brothers. They may be totally honourable, and be void of any negative or sexual thoughts. But your girlfriend might find it awkward. It is worse if you have a brother or brothers that are a bit of a pervert. Let's admit it, a lot of men are.

She wants you to have your own place where she can walk around naked if she pleases and be carefree.

No woman wants to go to her boyfriend's parents' house, and have sex for the whole family to hear. Really, it is embarrassing. Then when they bump into your mum, they get that look of disapproval or a smirk from your dad that says "I know what you were up to last night." Women generally tend not to enjoy that experience.

Do not be surprised if she stops having sex with you. Especially if somebody fails to knock and catches you in the act.

Primarily she wants to develop a relationship with you. Everybody else is peripheral to your relationship. She might not even want to meet your family until she decides that she likes you enough to meet them. If you are still at home with mummy and daddy - that may be a problem.

Grow up, save up and move out!

Big Baby

Some men cannot wipe their arses without the aid of their mothers or girlfriends. They cannot wash, cook, clean or do anything. They are nothing but big babies. I am serious, they are totally useless!

Their bedrooms have the same amount of minute species as the Amazon. For those of you that are unaware, the Amazon I am referring to is not an online shop where you can buy almost everything under the sun, the Amazon I am referring to is the largest rainforest on the planet, which is also home to a vast number of plants, insects and bacteria that go a long way to producing medicines and cures to all kinds of illnesses, infections and diseases. These guy's bedrooms are full of bacteria that could quite possibly be the next cure for Covid-19 or more than likely the next superbug that succeeds MRSA.

They would not know what clean looked like if it spat in their face. These grown arse men need to call mummy to ask how to use the washing machine yet they do not need a manual to operate a mobile phone.

These men walk around in un-ironed clothing because the last time they attempted to iron something they burnt it and nearly set the house on fire.

They do not know how to clean up after themselves. They put clothes on and take them off believing there is some magic fairy that will pick up their clothes and put it in the dirty laundry basket.

If and when they have a bath or a shower (I say if, because some men know very little about personal hygiene) they believe that porcelain has a self-cleaning mechanism so they never clean the bath or toilet behind them.

These guys are literally comfortable in their dirty and messy habitats. They will get drunk, vomit in their own bed and sleep in that same vomit for weeks unless someone helps them or changes their bedsheets for them.

I know some women are like, "who are these guys?" While other women are like "OMG, that is my boyfriend."

These rotten animals - also known as men - attract dirt and dust like flies on shit. They smell, their clothes smell and where they live smells. Yet they are immune to their own stink like a homeless person who cannot afford and does not have the means to improve their personal hygiene. Whereas these creatures do.

Unless someone cooks for them, these guys would starve. They are usually even too lazy to go to the shop to buy microwavable food or takeaway from a restaurant. They only started to feed themselves properly when all these online delivery companies appeared and saved them from death by malnourishment. They helped raise the value of Uber Eats and Just Eat single-handedly.

They can play COD or Fortnite all day every day and figure out the different modes and codes, but the washing machine or the cooker dials give them serious anxiety. They just about know how to use the microwave.

No matter how charming a guy comes across, if you go back to his house and the smell reminds you of raw sewage, run for your life unless you do not mind being his slave for the rest of your days or do not mind living in squalor yourself.

The problem with these lazy bums is that they expect women to be their mums. They cannot be bothered themselves, whether they are single or not, if there is a woman in their lives, they literally expect her to be his slave. Sorry mate, slavery was abolished worldwide in 1948.

How about you get off your sweaty bum and learn how to do some pretty basic stuff yourself. Need help? Ask Google, watch some YouTube videos, or buy a book and digest the information. A woman's role in life is not to be at your beck and call.

If you do happen to ask for her assistance, learn to ask nicely and appreciate whatever she does for you, as she does not have to do it. And return the bloody favour. You are no longer wearing nappies - unless you are - so act like it!

The Problems With Men

Man Flu

Men cannot even handle colds much less endure what a woman goes through. They are totally weak when it comes to any type of pain, especially if it is caused by some form of illness.

Some men, through bravado, will act as though they are not hurt if they are injured in a fight. Let them catch the flu, or get a headache, and see how weak and debilitated they become.

A lot of women go through tremendous pain and character altering hormone changes every month whilst the lining of their wombs shed.

They may also have to go through 9 months of pregnancy where an egg grows from a foetus into a full-grown baby. During those months they go through all types of aches and pains as their bodies go through all sorts of changes.

Then they have the painful pleasure and embarrassing experience of opening their legs in front of a bunch of midwives and potentially obstetricians during labour. They say who feels it, knows it. I cannot begin to imagine how physically painful any of those events actually are. Although I did watch Piers Morgan endure the pain of contractions after being hooked up to a labour simulation machine. It did not look like fun to me.

A man catches the flu and he acts like he has been shot or got norovirus.

Totally incapacitated.

Work is a myth. Leaving the bed is out of the question. According to him he needs looking after like a baby - a big baby. A man catches the common cold, and he can be completely incapacitated.

The common cold or the flu, or better named; man flu, does not alter any of your hormones as far as I am aware. It is definitely not a nice experience but it is one that only usually happens to many individuals two or three times per year.

Women have to endure their monthly cycle as the name suggests; monthly, for days at a time and they are not immune from catching a cold or the flu or any of the other pains or illnesses that men are accustomed to - but guess what? They just get on with it.

It is not just the flu that make men act like they are on their death bed. A man might get a headache and suddenly his world is likely to end.

As if to take the piss out of women's monthly suffering, if a man gets a stomach ache or suffers from diarrhoea, he acts like nobody else has survived such pain in their lives, whilst their wives and girlfriends, loving as they are, look at them with pity and look after them in their times of need, knowing the real pain they endure monthly.

Nearly all men want to be looked after in their moments of pain. They not only want, but they expect to be looked after like their girlfriend is a maid, a nurse and a doctor all in one.

Let the shoe be on the other foot and notice how empathetic, or more likely pathetic, a man becomes.

Unless a woman looks like she is about to die a man will think she can handle it. Even if she does look like she is about to die, he may still be uninclined to do much because he will believe she is exaggerating - because that is what he usually does.

One Trick Pony

Men can only do one thing.

One trick at a time. Well one thing at a time that is.

Other than that, they are totally useless!

Ask a man to do several things at once and watch his world fall apart. Not all men of course but in this instance, I would say the vast majority.

At the same time (excuse the pun), most women can do multiple things at once and many of them can do this with ease.

Not only can men only do one thing at time, but they cannot divert their attention to anything else whilst they are doing it. They cannot talk, in fact they cannot even listen at the same time, as any extra chore put on them is bound to lead them to error - for which you will most likely get the blame.

He was trying to concentrate but you spoke to him which interrupted his pathetic attention span and now he has made a mistake - or worse still, he has done it all wrong.

It is all your fault!

The Problems With Men

What a joke!

It is surprising that men can manage to breath whilst their heart beats at the same time. That must take some serious effort.

A man may actually ask for alone time to do something they simply cannot deviate their minds from, to give attention to anything else. The problem is some of the things they want to do take a lot of time.

A woman appreciates companionship. They love a man that can sacrifice some of their time for them but if a man needs a month to work on something then how are they meant to bond with him?

It is a wonder how so many men cheat. How can they deal with more than one woman at a time?

If a woman needs 5 minutes to do something watch how needy and annoying a man may become. All of a sudden you are the centre of their world. Whereas usually you may feel invisible to them. Now they cannot live without you. Understand this, a man needs to be left alone and all the time in the world to complete a task. If a woman needs a little time to complete a task, a man cannot accept that and begins to swarm the woman like bees on pollen; how dare she avert her attention to anything else but him?

Most men are one trick ponies and they only focus on one thing at a time, which can then lead to them compartmentalising things.

I was talking to a female relative of mine and she was complaining about her partner, who had cheated on her with another woman. The thing that bothered her the most, was that he had separated the two in his mind. For him, he was able to "put it in a box", with no connection between the two women.

Because he did this, his emotions were not clouded, but to her, she thought that he came across as cold and remorseless about being unfaithful. She could not fathom the idea of being in one box with one set of emotions, and the other girl being in another with a separate set of emotions tied to her partner. To her, this came across as if he felt no emotion towards the whole situation.

Although they broke up a considerable amount of time ago, that element of the set of circumstances still haunts her. It is something she cannot get her head around.

For a lot of women, the way that a man's brain operates does not make sense. They cannot comprehend distancing certain aspects of your life from another. And for them, that is a common problem with men.

Bromance

Ever notice how men act one way in front of their friends and another way when those friends are not around?

They put on all this bravado to impress the other guys around them. You look at him and wonder, who the hell is this guy? That is not how he acts when they are not around.

All of a sudden, he has got some super confidence because his friends are around. When they disappear, so does all that boldness.

Now you can slap him in his face with your dirty knickers and he will not say a thing.

When they are not around, he treats you like a princess. "Anything you want honey?" "Are you okay?" "Do you need anything darling?"

When his mates turn up it is more like, "get it yourself!" In fact, you turn into some slave for him and his cronies. "Get us this" and "get him that." It leaves you staring at this guy thinking, "who is this imposter?"

He looks the same. His voice sounds familiar. But his actions and behaviour are totally alien to the man that you are used to.

Then he wonders why you dislike his friends. He is totally bemused as to why you would not like his best pals.

Sometimes it is not all of his mates, just a select few or a select one. Usually that friend is in tight with him and encourages him to do all sorts of foolishness to your bemusement.

The loyalty between them is unquestionable. They treat each other better than they treat their girlfriends.

On the flipside of the problematic men above, you also have the men that treat their women like queens in front of the world. Everybody sees the way he treats her and is envious. They believe he can do no wrong.

When all his audience disappears, he turns into an obnoxious cunt. His tone changes. His manners are forgotten. He orders her about like a slave on the plantation fields. Leaving her feeling lost and in search of his friends to help him transform into the loving gentleman he was before they left.

Then you have the guys that spend all their time with their friends. You never get to see him because they are too busy having fun with Mike or Paul. He suddenly wants to spend time with you when he wants some sex. Tell him to go and fuck Mike or Paul because that is who he spends his time with.

Guys, if there is one thing most women cherish, it is companionship. They want you to spend time with them. You go out all the time with your friends so why can you not go out with her or, if the occasion is appropriate, bring her along. Make her feel involved. She might even decline the invitation, but she will appreciate that you thought of her and offered.

Guys pick all sorts of friends. Women will be more inclined to like your friends if your friends are in a relationship and are the committed type.

Some girls have kittens because their man's friends are either single and looking, or in a relationship and looking. She will be worrying that they will lead you astray. Unless, you are seriously committed and she can tell you most probably will be faithful. There is an old saying that goes "show me your company and I will tell you who you are". She does not want their frivolous behaviour rubbing off on you.

There is also the friend that can program your man like a computer. He seems to dictate your man's life. His influence outweighs yours, sometimes heavily. He may think very little of your suggestion, but when that mate says exactly the same thing, he does it without questioning anything. If you suggest something and his mate suggests the opposite, guess who wins that battle?

It may seem that your man cannot even think for himself. He does not make any decisions without his mate's approval. His mate literally owns your man like a puppy. He tells him what to do and say, whilst your man just wags his tail and follows orders. Yet your voice is nothing to be listened to.

You may want to alter how you say things to him if you fail to have any influence over him. Otherwise, just leave if it really bothers you or he fails to take heed.

Let us not forget the friend that tries his luck when your man is not around. He does not start off so boldly. It starts with just watching, he then tries a few sly comments to test the water. Comments that are not totally obvious.

They are comments that can easily be covered up as innocent. But really, he is seeing if you will go running to your man if he oversteps the mark.

When he feels it is safe, he goes one step further hoping that you will show him some interest. If you get mad and threaten to tell all, he counters with threats saying exactly the same. "I will tell him that you tried it on with me." He will say that you have only known him for 5 minutes, he has known him forever.

The Problems With Men

Guys be careful of the friends you keep. Pick them like you pick your fruit.

Men & Things

Some men treat their possessions like they are the most important things in the world, they will worship materialistic things and put them above people.

Ultimately, they will put all these worldly possessions above their girlfriends and wives and not stop to think of how unimportant that makes them feel.

Women want to feel special to their partner. They do not want to feel like they are second best or anywhere else thereafter.

A man will keep his car in immaculate condition but when his girlfriend asks him to clean up after himself in the bathroom for the hundredth time, he will carry on ignoring her or make minimal effort just to shut her up.

This can drive a woman crazy as she will think that you care more for your car than you do for her and the small requests, she asks of you.

He will spend more quality time with his phone or tablet in a day, than he does in a week with his partner. Then later, he will wonder why he cannot find these things because, out of the need to capture his time, his girlfriend will hide his prized possession(s).

This is likely to backfire because, instead of devoting quality time with her, he is now dedicating his time looking for his things. He will ask you to check one room while he checks another.

Another thing about a man's possessions is a lot of men will not let you touch them. Like you are a young toddler that is too young to touch such things. He will ban you from touching them which will usually only heighten your desire to play with them.

If he does let you touch them, he will monitor you like a prison guard supervising a family visit. Watching your every move to see exactly what you are doing. You will see the anxiousness on his face. It is as if he is in unbearable pain just waiting for you to hurry up and hand it back to him.

Then, just like that, he will be like "Okay that is enough!" grabbing the item from you with such aggressiveness that he nearly breaks it, and you, himself.

If you accidently damage or break a man's beloved possession, or even unintentionally reset his favourite device to factory settings, sometimes the fiery reaction in comparison to the actual mistake is gigantically out of proportion.

In that moment you can be forgiven for thinking that he may actually kill you.

He might.

Blaming at this present time, that young lady, is nothing but adding salt and vinegar to his open wound. Either the force of explosive anger may increase in volatility, or the silence may deafen you.

He will ignore you for however long it takes for him to get over it. In fact, a man can ignore a woman for so long that he may forget why he was ignoring her in the first place.

Sometimes there is just nothing you can do to console a man.

He needs his time to adjust to the new situation he finds himself in. The worst thing you can do at this point is belittle his favoured possession by saying something along the lines of "It is only a tablet" or whatever the damaged possession may be.

You may try to soften the blow by letting him know it was an innocent mistake.

It would be nice if a man could find the same love and devotion that he openly displays for his toys and gadgets and openly display that same love and devotion to his woman.

The Problems With Men

Some men do, whilst others fail miserably.

Mr Money

There is a famous quote apparently spoken by the Dalai Lama. When asked about humanity he responded with: "Man. Because he sacrifices his health in order to make money. Then he sacrifices his money to recuperate his health."

Some men do not have any time for women at all.

Why? Because time means money and they only have time for money. These men literally worship money. All they actually do is eat, drink and sleep money. If money is not involved, neither are they.

All their conversations revolve around money, or something connected with money. They do not have time for anything else.

They attract women because women (falsely) are attracted to these men's finances. They see their nice cars, fancy clothes or expensive watches, but when reality sinks in, and they realise there is nothing else to this individual, they are seriously put off.

Sometimes that reality takes a little time to sink in, but when it does finally sink in and they become immune to the riches due to the lack of substance in these men, it leaves them with a nasty hollow feeling inside.

So much so that their next boyfriend does not have much in his coffers, but has a lot more to his persona to compensate for it.

Some of these men do not even enter relationships. It is not that they are not into women, but the time involved in getting to know a woman is not worth it in their minds. These men would rather pay for sex than build a relationship with a woman.

They see that as a better investment of their time and money.

Some of them find very little time to find a girlfriend. But they think that a relationship consists of them putting money on the table. They think money alone will make a woman happy.

That is it.

They think their job is done.

They have no idea about women. It is true that some women are only interested in a man's wealth. They would make a perfect match for these men.

In reality, the vast majority of women are looking for meaningful companionship; good conversations and deep heart-warming memories. They want quality time with their partners.

Some women are not that interested in money at all. They are more interested in a man's heart and mind and want to spend some time with their man.

These guys spend the whole of their lives making their shekels and then they get old and turn around, looking for some female companionship. They do not even have the skillset to attract or keep a woman.

They end up attracting a blood thirsty gold digger who comes along looking for a place in his will. Whom then stresses him out so much, so that he dies soon after, as she exacerbates any bad health conditions he had. Or, creates some that he never.

Worse, is some of these men treat money like it is going out of fashion. Their bank accounts and assets say that their wealth is in good health. They may not necessarily be millionaires, but they are far from struggling financially.

These blokes turn out to be the meanest and stingiest guys on the planet. They make Jean Paul Getty look generous - the man who famously refused to pay kidnappers a ransom of $17m for his grandson, until they cut off his grandson's ear and sent it to him to make him aware of their seriousness. He paid a negotiated fee of $2.2m. He did not want to pay because he thought the sum was too high despite being a billionaire himself when very few existed.

These guys are rich (or comfortable at the least) but they are in love with money so much that they have the cheek to be stingy. It is as if they pay for a meal for two that all of a sudden, the whole of their wealth will disintegrate and they will be in debt.

Really attractive.

No doubt that women queue up around the corner trying to be with these men, only to find out that he is rich and that is the way it is going to stay. He will stay rich and you will still have whatever little, or big wealth you had when you met him.

If you think you are getting any of his money, forget about it. These men want to be buried with their money like Drake - literally.

Broke Bums

Girls, have you ever been out with a guy who has charmed the knickers off of you? Nicest guy on the planet. He knows just how to treat you; the sex is amazing - yet he does not take you anywhere.

That does not mean that you two do not go anywhere together, it just means he does not take you.

He may suggest that you go out somewhere together, and even choose the venue - but when the bill comes, it is you that is paying. He might go Dutch a couple of times, but in general it is you that foots the bill.

Sometimes it is because he is as tight as a virgin. He has got the cash but he does not want to spend it. This is not the stingy guy I am talking about - he is in the previous chapter.

The guy I am talking about cannot afford to take you out.

Fair enough, that a lot of us go through rough times financially at some point in our lives. A lot of us have been there. Life can be difficult monetarily. But unfortunately, when you are broke, you cannot afford a girlfriend. I myself have been told that by a previous girlfriend. I was in a low paid job just getting by, and that was my reality.

Not to say women are gold diggers. Not at all. The reality of life is that women cost money. Just as having children cost money. You would not say that an innocent baby is a gold digger, would you? But yet you still have to spend a hell of a lot of money raising a child. Nappies, cot, pushchair, pram, toiletries, clothes and food, to mention a few things you would have to spend on a baby, let alone when they get a little older.

Oh, you did not think that your child would survive on breast milk alone for the rest of their lives, or did you?

Many women are independent and do not need your money. The brutal facts of life are that life is expensive. It costs to live, unless you are a forager who lives out of bins and skips.

If you want to meet a woman, you may need to travel to meet her. That may consist of public transport, a cab, Uber, or you might ride or drive there. If you are riding a push bike, the bike (or rental of the bike) will cost you - unless you stole it. After your initial cost of that bike, travelling to and from will be free. But there is a cost involved.

Unless she is your next-door neighbour or she lives walking distance, it will cost you to travel to see her. The broke dude will try to get her around to his place. He most probably still lives at home with his parents because he cannot afford to live on his own.

It is a hard life but the facts of the matter are, most dates cost money and somebody has to pay. If you are a gentleman, it will be you. If you are a gentleman and you cannot afford it, you will take her somewhere free.

Do not get me wrong, many dates can be free. Walking is free. It is good exercise and it can be romantic too; such as a walk in the park or by the riverside. But there is only so much walking you can do. At some stage, somebody's belly is due to rumble because they are hungry or a drink might be needed to quench the thirst from all that talking you have been doing whilst you were walking.

McDonalds might work when you are a teenager. But as time goes on, women enjoy eating somewhere a bit more sophisticated, rather than sitting down with Ronald McDonald staring at them.

They are no longer 6 years old wishing for a Happy Meal.

Many women are understanding and will stand by you in your time of need. They may even support you financially during that time. But many will start to lose interest if you are not showing any potential financially. They saw potential in you when you first met, but now they are beginning to realise that that potential was something they dreamed of in their mind, but does not look like it is going to become reality.

Some of those women that stand by you will not mention it but in their mind, they will resent you. They will have friends and/or family members that are getting spoilt rotten by their partners and be envious of them.

Then they will come home to you. They will look at the bills that need paying, remember that it is them paying the bills, not you.

And they will feel like crying in despair.

Worst is the broke guy that expects you to look after him financially, yet he does not show any signs of improving his circumstances. He may be unemployed, but if he is not showing any willingness to look for a job, a woman will start to wonder what she is doing with him.

A lot of women do not have any time or patience for a man that is not making any or very little money. They will not even look in his direction.

They will be conversing and as soon as she finds out his financial position, her mind will switch off from the conversation. She may have been wetting herself with laughter 5 minutes ago, but now his voice is just background noise.

She can hear his voice, but she is no longer listening.

The most important thing to notice about a man that is penniless, is his mind-set. His mind-set does not consist of words alone that come from his sweet-talking lips, but also in his actions. If his words are positive and encouraging and his actions match, then he is likely to be going through a bad patch. But if he consistently cannot keep a job for longer than a month or two, then you have a problem.

Some women could not care less about a man's mind-set. Unless you are bringing home the bacon they are not sticking around. That is slightly unfortunate because money comes and goes.

For example, a man that knows how to make money, is used to making money loses his job, or an investment goes badly and he loses that outlay. But sooner or later, he will be back on his feet making money again. So do not write off all the broke guys in the world.

But if a man just talks about sorting out his financial affairs but does nothing to prove it, then unfortunately he is a bum with a bum's mind-set. If he does not even sound positive about his future merits, then there is a serious problem.

Stick with the guy that tries. Run a mile if he is not trying at all!

Online Dating

Online dating is plagued with weird men stalking, harassing, trolling and catfishing women. Not to say that it cannot and does not happen the other way around, but from what I have observed, to much less of an extent than what women are subjected to.

When I mention online dating, this is not exclusive to online dating apps. When a woman is on an online app where she has a profile with a picture, she then becomes a target for these relentless male predators whether she likes it or not.

These guys have not got any decorum, they do not even know what the word means. A woman may be on an online dating app and a man's first message may be something along the lines of, "I wanna cum in your face" or "Those lips look like they're made for sucking." There is not even a "hello, how are you? My name's Joe Bloggs" etc.

Just straight in with the nasty stuff.

You know what happens to these guys? More often than not they get blocked and deleted before they can send another message. They could have told a joke, or typed some cheesy chat up line, but they lack any form of creativity.

Many guys first message will be "Do you wanna fuck?" They will send the same message to every woman hoping for a positive response. They will feel hurt and disappointed when they face so much rejection. They may be lucky enough that one out of the 100 women that they send this message to is actually receptive to this kind of approach, only to find out that it is a bot or someone trying to catfish them.

Any real positive responses to this kind of message is likely to be very few and far between.

What men have to realise is, in the online dating world, women rule. They usually do not have to navigate the app and search for men. All they need to do is put up a couple of pictures and if they look half decent, the messages come flooding in.

Of course, on many of the dating apps now, you have to match, but for a woman to get a match it is not as hard as it is for most guys. Even the super picky girls get matches.

Guess what lads? A lot of women are super picky.

Online matching apps are made to feed into our superficial side. Matching is based upon looks predominantly, and we tend to become more finicky because there is more choice.

But many women will look at your pictures and read what there is of your bio. They are waiting to see something that catches their attention, that makes you stand out from the rest (in a positive light).

A lot of men on the other hand, just tend to look at the pictures and solely make their decision based on looks. That is, if they even make a decision. I have male friends who were on Tinder and they liked every profile they came across. They did not even look at the pictures, they just continually swiped right to try and get some matches.

With an inbox full up of matches and messages, a lot of women have a chance to choose who they are interested in. They do not have to settle for the messages with little effort.

I know it can be exasperating when you see a woman you like, you take the time to read her bio and then send a lengthy message which shows you read it, and that you have something more to say than "Hey" or "Hi, how are you?" Then unfortunately, you fail to get a reply. You might even get blocked and deleted. Then you come across many more profiles that you like and do something similar only to get little or no response.

Tough titty.

That is life, learn to deal with rejection my friend. It is part and parcel of the world we live in!

Yes, it is frustrating, tiresome and painful, but are you a man or a mouse? A woman does not have to like what you look like, they are not compelled to adore your approach or anything about you. We all like who we like. Just because you like anything in a skirt, does not mean that anything in a skirt is going to like you back.

Guys, do not be an imbecile all of your life! Most girls do not want to see a picture of your dick, especially when they have seen little, or none, of your character.

Most women are not desperate for sex, whilst in comparison quite a few men are. Even if a woman is desperate for sex, there are usually many men that will oblige. Unfortunately, the same does not always apply the other way around.

Remember, we are equal but different, men hold many advantages over women in other areas of life. When it comes to getting sex or attracting the other sex, women hold the cards. Do not cry like a big baby, that is just life and how it goes.

There are some women on dating apps that are selling sex for money, but they usually are upfront about it, or slyly suggest the fact.

The majority of women on these apps are not, and would rather that you did not offer them money for a pair of their worn knickers, or to meet them and indulge in sexual activities. A lot of women feel hugely offended by these messages.

Would you like to know the secret to meeting a woman online? It is quite simple - practice makes perfect. Forget the group photos, the blurred pics and the snaps where you are so far away from the camera that you look like Saturn (this actually goes for men and women).

Put up a photograph of your face that clearly shows your features, not too close so that people would have trouble knowing what they are actually looking at. Do not leave your profile with one picture either, you will come across as a catfish. Someone who is genuine should have more than one picture to put up. Put up another picture of your face from another angle so they get to know what they are looking at.

Also put up a picture which encompasses your full body. Make sure you have clothes on, it is not PornHub. This will allow people to see what your dress sense is like and if it is something they like. I think you should put up at least 4 or more pictures of yourself, but make sure you look decent in them.

And remember - no group picks. It is not a game of Where's Wally or Waldo?

Guys, remember what you are - a guy. Not a woman. Forget all these filters, especially SnapChat filters that obscure the viewer from seeing you properly, like a dog face with its tongue hanging out of your mouth. It is also annoying when women use them too. The whole point of pictures and videos in online dating is for your potential date to see whether they actually like the look of who they are considering dating.

If the app offers the chance to verify yourself then do so. You are trying to build trust in your potential date, being verified reassures them that you are the person they are eyeing up. But do not ignore the advice from above, that does not exempt you from putting up multiple photos. Still put them up!

Do not be stupid - do not upload pictures of another person and pretend to be them. Why on earth would you do that? I take it you intend to eventually meet someone in real life. They are going to notice that you are not the guy from the picture.

Men, women, we know you looked much hotter 5 - 10 years ago. The problem is you do not look like that now. Refrain from putting these pictures up unless you look the same. Your date will be disappointed when they meet you, and you will be disappointed when they block and delete you and you never see them again.

If you are unattractive, be creative. Take pictures until you look half decent. Some unlucky woman will eventually be interested in your ugly mug. It may take a while but good things come to those who wait and persist.

That means, if the app allows it, include some sort of a biography. This can be something imaginative, like presenting it as a job advert, but for a girlfriend or a wife. Or write about what you are looking for in a woman and write a little about yourself. Include things like whether you smoke, drink etc. Also include your height.

Do not lie about your height if you actually intend to meet this woman, she is going to realise how tall, or short, you really are. Be realistic, if you are 5 foot 5"/163cm you are unlikely to be successful with a woman who is 6 foot/183cm. It does not mean you cannot get a woman of that height, but your odds are short.

When messaging; be polite, creative, and witty. Pay attention to her responses and try and get a flow going that mirrors how she comes across. At the same time, you have to be yourself. There is no point in creating a completely different online character. Just like catfishing, if you fail to come across as the persona you have presented online, then she is unlikely to like you in real life. You want someone to like you for you, so be you.

Lastly - this is not mentioned much, if anywhere - is, approach women offline as well as online. Get used to being in the company of women you find attractive. Familiarise yourself with conversing with the opposite sex.

Too many men become keyboard daters, and flake on dates in real life because they are only used to talking to women online. They have not got any social skills in person and mumble, stutter, talk shit, fail to flirt, flirt badly, and/or speak inappropriately if and when they finally get their chance of a face-to-face date.

Then they turn around and blame women for their lack of a sex life. Do not be an incel!

Get a life!

Non-committed

Men just want to have their pussy and eat it. They may say they want to meet a woman and settle down but do they really mean it? A lot of females, from a young age, have dreams of getting married to their Prince Charming, creating a family and living happily ever after.

Many males, from a young age, dream of sleeping with as many women as possible - being a man-whore and being admired by their male counterparts.

Can you see how these two dreams do not match in matrimony?

In the back of men's minds, there may be a faint thought of settling down and having a family. Being man of the house and living happily ever after. But a lot of men are sexual beings, the thought of only sleeping with one woman for the rest of their lives may literally petrify them.

So, some men settle down, but they cheat.

Other men settle down, have a family, then somewhere along the line, decide to leave.

Whilst other guys never settle down, or start to think about it when they can see deaths door around the corner.

You do get men that settle down, do not cheat and stay committed until death. But they are hard to find, or they may have multiple deficiencies, so they stay because nobody else would have them.

They are either ugly, stupid, broke, have communication problems, or a combination of these and all the rest highlighted in this book muddled into one person.

Yes, that is right - they might be your worst nightmare, and in that case, the woman might cheat or leave instead.

It is in a woman's interest to stay with the father of her children. She wants the model relationship. Women feel a sense of achievement when their relationships are fulfilling. She does not want to feel like she has failed at family life, she wants that environment for her children. That is why many women stay with men that do not particularly add to their happiness. They stay with a man that cheats on them or is abusive to them in some shape or form, because they want the relationship to work. They put their all into making it work.

Men on the whole feel fulfilled when they are successful in their careers and are making a good amount of money. They are trying to make enough money to make sure that they can feed themselves and any dependents they have. His motivations might not necessarily be financial, but he will want to achieve his goals and strive towards his dreams.

For many a woman, having a husband and a family is their ultimate goal. Business, career, or a childhood hobby-cum-adult fixation is a lot of men's ultimate dream. The money is still important to women as they want stability, but it is usually secondary. Many men do want a wife and children, but again, for men that may be secondary.

If a woman has decided to be in a relationship with you, she will usually work at fixing any problems that come up, while the relationship is still alive.

Many men are noncommittal until it is too late. Their woman is fed up of their bullshit and ready to move on. Then out of the blue, this guy is ready to die for her.

Where was that commitment when it really mattered?

Now you have allowed her to build up multiple resentments towards you. You might still win her over, but she may be quite a handful to be with until she builds up trust for you again - which could take years. She may have many demands that she expects from you now that she is ready to leave. She may never get over her resentments and you may never hear the last of them.

Then again it might be too little too late. Sorry, but she may have had enough.

We are not here for a long time. Make the most of your opportunities. If you meet someone who makes you feel good inside and fills your heart with love, do not take them for granted. You may be surprised at how difficult it can be to find someone that touches your heart in the same way.

Sperm Donors

Most men want children but a lot of them do not want to do the hard work that is involved. I am not talking about the fun part. I am talking about the real nitty gritty stuff.

Why? Because they cannot be bothered.

They will turn around and say that is a woman's job, or make up some other flimsy excuse, but the truth is these men do not have the will or want to wake up in the middle of the night and change their baby's nappy, amongst other things.

Children are hard work. There is no doubt about that; looking after a child is tiresome. It can be absolutely exhausting. This is not always recognised by men in society. They think it is a doddle.

They believe the real hard work is done when you have to leave the house and go to work.

Wrong!

Looking after children and maintaining the home is as difficult as it gets. Just take a look at the animated film The Incredibles II (sorry if I have spoiled the plot). When a man has to do everything in the house; the housework, cooking, looking after the children etc., standards may easily begin to drop dramatically, and that is when a man can empathise with the real struggles mothers (and the odd father) across the world have to go through on a day to day basis.

After the blissful moments in the bedroom and the 9 months of waiting (it is actually calculated in weeks but you get the gist), a beautiful child is finally born. Everybody has fallen in love with this new baby - most of the time (not all of the time, some mothers suffer from post-partum depression and some fathers are just not interested).

Then when it is daddy's turn to hold the baby, daddy is more than happy to oblige until the baby starts crying. He may try a few tricks, but when those fail, he is ready to hand the baby back to the mother.

Great stuff.

The same thing may happen if there is an awful smell lingering in the air that does not seem to be going away anytime soon. He looks at the mother and hands the baby over like the child has nothing to do with him.

Do not get me wrong, you do have some new-age fathers who are willing to do their fair share, but worldwide, women bear the brunt of the responsibility when it comes to children.

Again - men want children, they may have convinced a reluctant woman into having a child with them, or for them. Then, for some reason, they end up knowing next to nothing about their own child. They are likely not to know the nappy size, or their shoe size. They do not know what foods they like or dislike.

Every time they need to purchase something, they have to ask the mother a million and one questions because they know nothing about this child that they wanted so badly.

Some men even forget their own children's birthdays. They need reminding and updating about everything, because they are clearly not interested enough to remember anything important about their own children.

Then, if by some sudden miracle they remember something important, these fathers feel so proud of themselves. They highlight the fact that they remembered something worth remembering about their own child.

Whoopee doo.

Many mothers remember everything about their children and they still find space in their memory banks to remember everything about the father too.

Then there are the non-existent fathers who get a woman pregnant and do not even stick around. These unfortunate women never see these men again. They are gone with the wind - literally.

Some stick around and try to make things work, but they up and leave when they are ready, and then they become part-time fathers, seeing their children every other weekend or every so often.

That is, if you are lucky. Some guys start up a new family and forget they had any children before. They do not just forget birthdays; they forget their children completely.

Women have to watch their children go through the pain of losing a father. Maybe see the father disappoint them by being late when they are around, or not turn up at all.

If you only see your child once a week or fortnightly, how hard can it be to turn up or be on time? To some so-called fathers, it is the hardest thing ever.

It is fair to say that not all relationships work out, sometimes because of timing, sometimes because people are not suited. Sometimes it is better for the parents to be apart because they cannot get along, and staying together could end up damaging any children involved because of the toxic state of the relationship.

One of the worst situations a woman can find herself in, is with a child or children for a man that she is no longer with, but yet he wants to wield power like he is still her man.

He will order her about, like she belongs to him. Sometimes he will use the children to control her. For instance, if she does not have much of a support network, then he will take advantage of that fact. If she wanted to go out but needed childcare, he would refuse to look after his own children for the night, then, he can dictate when and where she goes. These fearful sperm donors do this to prevent the mother of their child finding somebody new.

He might not look after them at all, for this reason alone.

They will also use money to restrict the mother's activities.

He may no longer be with her, but he still wants to control her life.

Some men just cannot bond with children. They think their job is to supply the sperm and money and their job is over. They are present but absent.

They may leave the house early and get home late. They hardly see their children even though they live in the same house. The children may see their daddies from time to time, but the fathers do not actually make an effort to bond with their child. They never get to know each other, leaving a hole in each other's lives.

Unfortunately, these children miss out on an important relationship with their old man and thus, it can complicate relationships and friendships later on in their lives, because they did not receive any love from their dads.

I am not talking about paedophilia. I am talking about that father-child relationship where a father acts like a father. Shows them love, teaches them things, guides them through life, plays games with them and spends meaningful time with his child or children. So much is gained when this happens and so much is lost when it does not.

What a shame.

Then you have the fathers that do not want to pay a penny for their child's upbringing. Getting money out these men is like getting blood out of a stone. Some men prefer to make sure the child has everything they need. They provide clothing, food and toys etc. but this is usually because they do not trust the mother.

Others are just not willing to part with any of their hard-earned cash. You have to call in the CMS or take them to court to get anything out of them.

Otherwise forget it.

Bastard

Who said men are not bitchy? Because many of them are. Except we do not call them bitches - we should, but we do not. We call them bastards.

Many men are as spiteful as can be. It is not widely reported, but men can be as emotional as women and just as spiteful. Need I point to the 45th president of the so-called Free World for example. But he is not alone. We are surrounded by these men, who are emotional wrecks, chat behind people's back, then smile in their faces. They use different terminology for men, they call them snakes or something along those lines. If a woman does it, she is bitchy, but it is the exact same thing.

Hurt a man and he will hurt you back. Some women may lack the physical strength of their male counterparts, so she will hurt you with her mind whereas a man is more likely to use his physical strength to lash out.

Many men will hold a grudge instead and hurt you in some other way when you least expect it. It happens in politics; a male dominated area, it also happens in the workplace and in our personal lives too.

A man would sleep with another man's woman, not because he likes her, but for some twisted, bitter revenge he has been dying to administer.

Men can be very competitive. They will ruin everyone else's lives, including their own, just so they can get that sense of winning. They can be horrible creatures. A man will burn down his own house and everything in it simply so his rival can get in trouble for arson.

Women may not notice this bitchiness so much because it is usually directed at other men. But women can become the target of their vindictive behaviour, if she ends up tangled in his web of malicious thoughts by stepping on his toes. He may cover his tracks well, but the nasty side of him will come out when it is good and ready.

A man can become as evil as he wants when the time comes. Just look at the size of the prison population and the ratio of men to women. Look at all the wars across the planet for so many centuries. It is not usually women starting these wars or leading the armies. How many women are the head of the army in their country? Not to say women are not capable but if we lived in a woman's world would armies even exist?

They blame violence on human nature, but I am not sure I would call it that. I would be inclined to call it male nature. Yes, women can be violent but no way near the same scale as men. You have your exceptions to the rule, like former British Prime Minister Margaret Thatcher, going to war with Argentina over the Falkland's Islands, or Islas Malvinas as it is known in Argentina.

But for every Margaret Thatcher, there is 1000 warlords, commander's in chief, terrorists or just plain old violent criminals that were born with the XY chromosomes.

Sad to say, but the world is full of bastards.

Control Freaks

Men want to control everything. And I mean everything. They want to control the weather, the earth, the sun, the universe. They use all sorts of technology to control everything around them.

Computers, phones, televisions, even traffic lights control our behaviour and most of these technologies are built by men. In the early days of computers women made up the lion's share of the job market as it was considered a woman's job. As time has gone by, if you look around the technology sector, it is mostly built and controlled by men.

While any individual has the capacity to control what they do and say, you cannot completely control others - although that does not stop many men from trying. I say completely control, because some people seem to have the ability to control others, as seen in the Stanford Prison Experiment and many other scenarios.

Governments, an area largely dominated by men, control countries and influence behaviour through laws, policies, tax incentives, tax disincentives, advertising campaigns, speeches, statements and all different ways through media and propaganda to influence people's ways of thinking and actions.

Men in general are control freaks. Worst of all they want to control women. They want to tell a woman what she can and cannot do and when she can and cannot do it.

Women have brains. They are capable of making their own decisions and knowing what is best for them. Yes, some women can be indecisive, they can also change their minds frequently, but that is their choice.

Men on the other hand, tend to forget that women are actually human beings with their own independent thoughts. Men think they know best and think that they are always right, even when they are wrong. Their egos will not allow for anything else.

These men will stifle a woman's life trying to control her every move; what she wears, what she eats, where she goes and who she hangs around with etc. Some women like a little friendly advice, but most do not want a dad for a boyfriend, bossing them about and restricting every aspect of her life.

There are men that genuinely care about their woman, and are only trying to uplift them and help them be their best selves. They give advice on what choices she should make, because they honestly are concerned about her.

Some women are looking for reassurance in their decisions, or approval because they care about what their man thinks of them. It does not automatically mean they want to be bossed about.

Just because a man says something does not mean she is going to do what he says. What men do not comprehend, is that many women tend to accommodate their man by appeasing him because she adores him and is trying to satisfy him. She may want to please him to make him happy, but she is making that choice.

If she feels uncomfortable doing something, she may say no or not do it if she is being nice. Or she might tell you to go and fuck yourself!

The truth about these pitiful men is that, the reason they try to control women is because they feel so out of control on the inside. They find order in controlling things and others. They are insecure, and more than likely petrified of losing her. They do not know how to act in any other way, so they act with a fake air of authority and attempt to govern her every move.

We all want to feel valued. Whereas showing that you care by looking out for a woman is an admirable thing to do. Trying to control and manipulate a woman like a puppet can lower her self-esteem, own belief in herself and affect her morale.

This may make her feel like a prisoner - and one day she may just decide to rebel. Unfortunately for him, he will have very little control, if any at all, as to how she rebels.

She may ignore you, do the opposite to what you say, or she may meet up with another man and do as she pleases. He is likely to be completely different to you, because anything that reminds her of your ridiculous, domineering, insecure self, is likely to leave her with a sick feeling in her stomach, and I do not mean butterflies. She might actually leave you for him.

Goodbye.

She will not necessarily need a man to move on, she might just have had enough of your bullshit and up and leave like Keyser Söze - never to be seen again.

And just like that, she is gone.

Mr Abusive

Sometimes you enter a relationship, and you have visions of grandeur of what you want the relationship to be, or what you want your partner to be like. When the relationship and that partner fail to live up to your expectations, you complain.

You expected so much more.

That relationship did not meet your expectations, but your partner was respectful, they cared, they tried. You felt safe. You felt looked after.

You become conditioned into getting the basic comfortability you got from that relationship, and blindly assume that that is what you will get with the next person you meet. You believe you will be respected and will feel safe in this relationship.

Why would you not?

This new person excites you, just as many new relationships start off with a buzz. Everything is going great as far as you are concerned.

One morning he wakes up early, to go to work as usual, you hold him back and ask him to stay a little while. His reply is brutal punches that leave you shocked, disorientated, hurt, and bruised. He gets ready to go to work as if nothing out of the ordinary has happened.

You are left to think about life.

As this behaviour was unprovoked but also out of the norm, you wonder why it occurred? What did you do that made him want to hit you? You look inwards to find answers. It was an irrational reaction, so you think about it irrationally, because thinking about it logically does not make sense. Instead of seeing that he has a problem, somehow you find a way to blame yourself for his hideous behaviour.

Let us get this straight, it was not your fault!

He has a problem. He is a fucking idiot!

For whatever reason, some buffoons think it is okay to abuse women. Sometimes it is inherited from the household they grow up in, other times it is cultivated in their social circles and made to seem normal. Sometimes it is part of the culture of their country of origin.

Regardless of where the seeds of disrespect are grown, it is wrong!

Women can be difficult at times. They can be argumentative, annoying, clingy - they can knowingly or unknowingly get on a man's nerves. They can even be spiteful.

That does not mean that they deserve the heart-breaking turbulence that being in an abusive relationship brings. Nothing justifies the emotional, verbal, and physical maltreatment that many of them face in these so-called partnerships.

Some pathetic fools, when frustrated, seem to only be able to articulate themselves angrily or abusively. Instead of finding the patience to speak with respect to their partners they admonish them belligerently.

Some only do it in private, others only do it in front of an audience. Others care little for who is present or not and dispense their diatribe in a careless manner.

The recipient may feel totally embarrassed with this disrespectful verbal tirade which is administered in front of others. They feel belittled and unappreciated. Whether they argue back or not, these onslaughts are hard to forget and are banked in their memory cells.

These feeble excuses for men verbally abuse their partners to make them feel small, but to ultimately make themselves feel larger than they really feel inside.

When the truth is, they feel inadequate.

The problem with these worthless creatures, is in their failure to control their own emotions and insecurities, they decide to attempt to control others in a negative manner. They ignore a woman when they cannot get their own way.

They get physically violent to administer their will by force. They want to be a force to be reckoned with, because deep inside they feel insignificant.

Because they are insignificant.

In order to maintain control, they play all sorts of mind games to gain power.

If you are a woman and you find yourself in one of these relationships, get out!

Do not subject yourself to the humiliation or the trauma that these situations generate.

One of the women I interviewed on this subject, left the father of her child barefoot, with the clothes on her back, her son and some of her son's belongings.

It took her a while to get back on her feet, but she got out alive.

Others are not so lucky...

A woman I once knew passed away. I was told that she was killed by the father of her children, who also suffered abuse from him. The last time I saw her, she was on the run from him, hiding in women's refuges as he had hit her and their twin children.

Some men have been abused, bullied, or thrown into traumatic situations themselves which leaves them stunted in their capacity to deal with life.

Nobody cares what you have been through once you start abusing women. There is no excuse.

The problem with men is they can be angry and aggressive. Frustrated with parts of - or all of - their lives, not knowing how to handle their emotions, many of these barbarians tend to lash out at the people closest to them.

Instead of looking within, or possibly seeking help, many men would rather verbally abuse or physically attack their beloved women, that are just looking to love and be loved.

They seek to control their woman like an animal, instead of as an independent companion. Some men treat their pets better than they treat their girlfriends. Some actually practice animal cruelty too.

Men in their younger years tend to be full of testosterone, vying, sometimes fighting, for their place in the world. In their battle to step up the ladder of hierarchy amongst their peers, they pick up habits and traits that may not make them the best of people to be close to.

People pick up habits, whether those be considered good or bad. Once they become a long-term habit, then it becomes part of that person's behaviour. If a man's habits or transitioned behaviour have been to dominate his surroundings in an abusive manner, then whoever is close to him will feel his wrath.

Regrettably, that is usually his girlfriend.

A lot of the time there are not any red flags. A woman meets a man who is charismatic and charming. He gives her that warm feeling inside. She is always delighted to see him and be in his company.

He is waiting to reel her in, whether that be consciously or subconsciously. Once he feels that he has her at his whim, the liberties he takes hit her like a brick wall.

How weak must you be to take someone's complete love and devotion and abuse that?

Abuse comes in many forms. An innocent woman encountering harsh verbal abuse for the first time can become shellshocked and hide in her shell. Emotional abuse can scar for life. Physical abuse can leave a woman in serious pain with cuts and bruises as memorabilia and a traumatised mind that finds it hard to get over the emotional turmoil.

Women want to enjoy life. They want to be loved and desired, and when they get what they consider to be the sought-after attention they so desperately wanted, they grasp onto the provider with all the adoration and love they have to give.

It is not always reciprocated.

She can end up feeling trapped in a relationship that she believes she cannot get out of safely. From the paradise in her mind, to the dungeons of reality she then finds herself in.

She can feel like she is walking on thin ice, not knowing if the next step is going to be the fatal one that breaks his non-violent demeanour into a raging flurry of abuse.

Another woman told me her story. She was pregnant with her partners' children (she was expecting twins). He punched her and kicked her down the stairs. While she suffered an emotionally draining and physically painful miscarriage, he went to sleep as if nothing had happened. She told me this roughly 15 years after it had happened, but she spoke with such tearful emotion, I could tell it still haunts her like it happened yesterday.

These soulless psychopaths deserve the gutter.

When you are abused, it can shock you and leave you disorientated and unsure of what to do or how to deal with the situation. While you are still trying to figure out what is going on, the abuse persists, and continues to blunt your reactions and thought process.

It takes a while for your mind to fully process the sequence of events and rationalise what you underwent. This can take years, decades, sometimes a lifetime. Some people die before they come to terms with what happened to them.

Many are left stunted in their growth as a person, never quite trusting others and/or themselves again. Many can become hostile themselves whenever they feel threatened. Some are unrecognisable as the person they once were before the abuse.

There is a lot of damage left behind in the wake of these thuggish beasts.

A woman is singing a song recently sent to her by her friend. They have known each other since childhood. She has since deleted the message but listens to it on the internet when her partner is away. He comes home and hears her singing the song.

"Where do you know that song from?"

She looks up at him in silence, frantically thinking of a reasonable answer in her mind.

"I have never heard that song before and I haven't heard you sing it before."

He watches her every move like a director on a film set. Anything she says or does that he is unaccustomed to is cause for suspicion. Today she is lucky he has chosen not to hit her. Yet, she is not relieved, as she is still unsure as to whether he is going to change his mind and switch on her.

Unfortunately, this is a daily occurrence for many women. Living in fear of what their partner is going to do.

This is a man that is full of insecurities. Clearly, he did not get enough attention in his childhood.

Grow up!

Most women with children tend to feel a responsibility to set a good example for their offspring to follow. When a woman is in an abusive relationship, she may feel torn between maintaining the family life that she wants her children to experience and grow up in and leaving the family unit environment because she does not want her children to see her suffer in an abusive relationship.

After enduring the abuse, she is likely to feel guilty and ashamed. If you are one of those women, forgive yourself.

Unfortunately, you got caught up in a relationship that was not the best for your mental health or any children you may bear. But we are not perfect. We live, we experience, and we grow. We are born innocent and we cannot know how to deal with every situation that comes our way in the perfect manner. We cannot always foresee what we later see in hindsight. That is life and the ugly beauty of it all.

Children growing up in a violent household can become accustomed to the violence they witness. They can become violent themselves. Children tend to play out what they see. The effects of your behaviour can have repercussions that last a lifetime.

You cannot predict the effect any event or prolonged experience will have on children. Witnessing abuse from a young age can leave a child with trust issues as well as normalising violence. Others may become withdrawn from life and become a shadow of their former selves.

Some children may not show any signs of indifference to the state of affairs but that does not mean that it did not affect them, or that it may not appear later on down the line. But you may fail to make that connection because of the time that has lapsed.

Men need to be aware of the monsters they may create. Some will be repulsed by the reflections of themselves they see in their children.

This is not to say that children cannot be resilient, and we all find our own ways to deal with the challenges that life throws at us. Some cope better than others.

Physically, men tend to be built stronger than women. Not always, but it is the general rule of thumb. Men tend to get into physical altercations more than women too, so their practice in physical fights is usually more than a woman's. These are some of the reasons why it is unacceptable for a man to hit a woman.

Some women will fight back when a man hits them, but the sheer physical imbalance makes it hard for them to win.

I spoke to women who suffered various levels of abuse, from a woman that experienced emotional abuse, including gaslighting, a lady who had encountered verbal abuse, a female who endured physical abuse 3 times within a 7-year relationship, to women that withstood constant abuse of all forms, including rape over numerous years.

I did not just gather information by interviewing women for the purpose of this book. Unfortunately, I have come across many women who I have spoken to over the years that have been subjected to all sorts of abusive situations and relationships.

Perverts

Men are perverts. If they did not have to work, they would most probably spend all day at home watching porn, or worse than that, go out and perv on women in the real world.

These pathetic excuses for men either lack the confidence, ability, or both, to approach women with respect and manners. They either whistle, holler crudely from afar, or say nothing at all. But what they do do, is stare at every woman that passes their way. They tend not to focus on a woman's face for too long, if they do at all.

The problem with these men is they gaze at women's bodies all day every day. They find it hard to remove their attention from women's breasts, bottoms, or their legs. Some of these men will attempt to look up women's skirts on escalators either shamelessly or sneakily. Others 'upskirt' them on their innocent journeys to and from places and go home to wank at the footage they have captured if they do not get arrested.

No woman likes to be upskirted.

Some women like attention, but few want a man to glare at her breasts whilst they are in conversation, forgetting that she has eyes that can see what his eyes are doing.

A lot of men have no filter when they speak to a woman. You can hear their disgusting thoughts right off the bat. They disclose their vulgar thoughts that you would assume they would save in a private file in their brain.

Unfortunately, the repulsive words roll off their tongues like a truck driving high-speed without apology. They either fail to notice how awkward they are making the female recipient feel, or they just do not care. Some of these simpletons actually get a rise from making a woman feel squeamish.

A woman I know used to be revolted by her ex-boyfriend. He was not only a complete pervert with her, but also with her female friends. She told me that when she used to exercise, he would ask her to do it naked, then he would get close up and look at her genitals, fascinated. At first, she did not think much of it but when it continued throughout her relationship with him, she found herself detesting him and his perverted behaviour.

She also told me of incidents where he would say inappropriate things to her girlfriends or harass them blatantly in front of her. They once picked up her friend and when she got in the car, he told her he loved her breasts. She told me she could feel how uncomfortable her friend felt and she herself felt totally embarrassed by his behaviour. This was just one of the many depraved things he had done unashamedly through the course of their relationship.

But guess what? She is not alone. Many men talk and act like this because they are perverted by nature. To them, this is normal.

Please do not be surprised, one of the most searched for terms on the internet is porn, and the names of porn websites. Men can miss a date because they could fail to take themselves away from wanking, watching porn.

Instead of switching it off to go and meet a real woman, they end up being late or missing the date entirely because they could not draw themselves away from a woman they will never meet or see in real life, unless they go to a porn event where they are unlikely to get to touch any of the pornstars there anyway.

Great stuff.

If and when some of these men do get into relationships, they make their woman feel inferior, as they watch vast amounts of porn instead of spending time with their woman. Because porn is their go to for sex, the type of sex they want to have with their woman may be questionable, at the least. Some women are fine with what these men are asking for, but many women feel nauseous at the suggestion of him eating her out whilst she is on her period or asking to piss on her.

Yuck!

It takes all sorts of people to make the earth go around, but really?

Sex

A lot of men seem or try to act emotionless until they ask a girl a question that they think they want to know the answer to. But they really do not want to know.

Unfortunately, they only realise that they do not want to know the answer when they find out the answer.

Normally they act as if they are as hard as nails then they ask a girl a stupid question like, "how many men have you slept with?" When the answer comes back, they look as if they want to cry. You can see it in their eyes, the window to the soul. From He-Man they fade into Cringer and cry like a baby. They may not actually cry, but girls can tell that they want to. The tears are hiding but they are dying to come out and roll down their cheeks.

Some men react angrily or aggressively as the shock brings it out of them, whilst others will try and put the girl down, or say some sarcastic comments with a lot of truth hidden in their jest. This answer may haunt them for months, some men years. Some men cannot ever get over it. Some actually leave the relationship because it is too much for their inflated ego.

That is one of many stupid questions asked by men when they clearly are unable to handle the reply. Some men ask who has given their girl her best sex, or who has been their most endowed partner.

They are not emotionally equipped for the truth. Some girls realise this and bend the truth or blatantly lie. Others tell the truth and shoot him in his heart with their response by just being honest.

Guys, you have to realise you are not the only man on the planet. A girl may have been with a guy or guys before you came along. If you are not built with the mental maturity to deal with answers that do not match your ideal, or what you are anxiously hoping the answer to be: do not ask the questions. It is pretty easy.

Prevention is better than cure.

Most men do not need any reason to have sex. They do not need any props. The mood and atmosphere are all meaningless or extras that are unimportant to many men. The opposite can be said for a lot of women. They like the mood set, the lights dimmed or off, or scented candlelight flickering in the background, because they are selective beings.

Most women will have sex for the following reasons (there may be other reasons, but these will be the most prevalent ones), in no particular order:

1. If she feels connected to a man and the mood/moment is right.
2. If she is on the rebound from a past relationship. There may be many underlying reasons for this, such as revenge or a feeling of rejection.
3. If she is intoxicated with drugs and/or alcohol and her inhibitions are lowered (or non-existent).
4. If she is horny, for any reason.
5. If she is feeling guilty for some reason related to her sexual partner, such as she has not had sex with him for a while and he keeps going on about it (she may also refuse sex for the same reason, whining men are not attractive to women unless they are called Shabba Ranks - that is a joke by the way).
6. Make up sex.

Have you ever seen those old Tom & Jerry cartoons, where Tom the cat looks at Jerry the mouse and sees Jerry as a steaming roasted chicken served up on a plate, ready to be eaten?

That is how a lot of men see women, but instead of a delicious meal served up, ready to eat, a man will see a fully clothed woman and imagine a woman naked lying on a bed with her legs invitingly akimbo, waiting for him to mount her, or whatever sexual position he prefers.

Even if that is not what he envisions, that is what a lot of men make women feel like.

All they care about is sex.

He will talk about it like it is the latest trend on Twitter. He will be impatient like a child pestering their parents for the latest toy. He will play all sorts of mind games to get it.

As soon as the opportunity presents itself, he will rush to get it, like a queue for toilet paper when coronavirus unleashed itself on the world.

He will feel like a King.

She may well feel used like a prostitute.

Then he will roll over and fall asleep while she will be longing to be hugged and comforted.

He did not even know how to take time and get her in the mood, just jumped right in while she was still dry downstairs, not in the mood and otherwise engaged, or with something else occupying her mind. Though, some women like the element of surprise.

There is a myth that women do not like sex but that is what it is - a myth. Many women love sex. Most women love to be made love to. The thing about sex is it is usually not the most important thing in a relationship to a woman. That does not mean that it is not important, it is just not the be all and end all for a lot of women.

To a man, sex is top priority. They act as if they are going to die if they do not get it. Sex is like oxygen to men. As if a woman is torturing them if they do not get any.

You have to learn to understand women, particularly your woman. People like to shop and buy things, but nobody wants to feel like they have been sold to. They want to feel comfortable with their decision. Not tricked into sleeping with you.

For a man sex is one thing, the act of sex itself. Putting his willy in and wiggling it about until he cums.

To women, sex is like a 3 course or a 5-course meal. There is the build-up before anything sexual even occurs. That could be engaging conversations over a period of time, whether throughout the day or for the last couple of weeks, building up an emotional connection.

It could be you two spending the evening together or going out creating a romantic atmosphere. Most women, if not all, like to feel connected mentally and emotionally to the man they are having sex with.

Then there is the foreplay. Looking into each other's eyes, flirting, and talking. The kissing, touching, hugging, licking and sucking. All the things that give a woman goose bumps. The whole world knows that you cannot wait to shove your dick inside her, but foreplay is something that helps make a woman feel aroused and valued.

The problem with men is they tend to rush this bit. They act as if sex is going to go out of fashion if they do not start penetrating her straight away.

Take your time.

Sex is not just about the physical act; it is everything encapsulated. The more you stimulate a woman's mind the more she is likely to desire you. The more pleasurable and stimulating the foreplay is, the better the sex is likely to be for her. And the more likely she is to lose herself in the moment. The more she enjoys herself, the more likely she is going to want to have sex with you again and again and again.

Foreplay is not an exact science, as every woman is different - although many women may enjoy similar things. Foreplay and sex in general are like art. Art is subjective. You need to learn how to handle your woman by trial and error, but the more errors you amass with a specific woman the more likely she is to be turned off by you.

Explore her body and remember to pay attention. If her face looks like, "What the fuck are you doing? I don't like that", then do not continue doing that. If she moans and groans, or even better her eyes roll to the back of her head, then you are likely to hit the jackpot, but do not only do that every time, find other things that evoke a similar reaction.

Women, you need to do men a favour in this department, do not fake it when you dislike something, especially overdramatically when you feel that you would rather that he stops. Emphasize your enjoyment more when you actually like the things he is doing.

Also, I know a lot of you like having sex in the dark for whatever reasons but having sex in the light allows a man to read you better. A lot of men seem to have emotional agnosia - a condition that affects the ability to perceive facial expressions, body language and voice intonation. As this is the case, men need all the help they can get.

Some men are awful kissers. They suck a girl's tongue so hard she feels like her tonsils are going to be sucked out from the back of her throat. Or they bite her lip like they are trying to crunch a Gobstopper or Jawbreaker. Stop it, it is not nice. Other men's kisses are too wet and sloppy, she does not want to feel like she is drowning in your slobber. Or their lips are like barbed wire, as dry as sand and ready to cut up any lips they encounter.

Other men have poor kissing technique. For example, there are ways to use your tongue when kissing. Shoving your tongue down a girl's throat and making her feel like you are choking her is not always one of them. It is a matter of delicacy and skill, not to mention passion.

As with many men, they are far too interested in their own pleasure to notice that the woman they are kissing is not enjoying the experience.

Some men's oral hygiene is so disgusting that kissing them is out of the question. In other words - their breath stinks.

Brush your teeth and your tongue!

Nobody wants to be kissing dragon breath. It is horrendous. If your breath does not smell too polite, you must know. If you know, do something about it. The same goes for your overall hygiene.

Do not ask for sex. That is right, sex is not something you ask for. Yes, with all the laws surrounding consent it may be scary to know if and when it is okay to have sex with a woman but do not ask. I am a strong believer that sex is something that just happens when the time is right.

The moment you ask for sex, is the moment you will become unattractive to many women. If you were in with a chance, it is likely that you just fucked it up. Read the situation; if you face resistance or she tells you no, stop right there, you clearly read the situation wrong. She will either; be thrilled that you like her in that way and want to take it further, but she might not be ready just yet or, she will be utterly repulsed that you even thought that she thought of you in that way or anything in between. Either way, her reaction will speak wonders.

To some women the thought of being fingered will make them vomit and they are not stimulated in this way. Others are sexually awakened by the thought alone. Let us be fair here, a lot of men do not have a clue as to what they are doing or what they are supposed to be doing in this area. That is okay if you are a teenager still learning the ins and outs of sex, but if you are older, you are expected to know what you are doing. If you get this wrong you could seriously injure a woman, if you get it right you could give this woman the best, or in some cases the only, orgasm she has ever had.

All of this takes trial and error with each woman a man encounters. The way you play with her sexual organ will differ depending on the woman. Just like goldilocks and the 3 bears, not too hard not too soft but just right, or not too fast not too slow - you catch the drift.

Your hands need to be clean or you might accidently affect her PH levels and give her thrush. Make sure the area is lubricated as the dry friction may feel like you are rubbing sandpaper down there. If you use your spit make sure you have brushed your teeth. If you have been eating hot peppers, this might still be in your saliva and will burn her like a bush fire in Australia.

Imagine driving a manual car trying to get to your destination and the car keeps running into traffic and having to stop. Every time you stop, you have to start off in 1st gear and build your way up. All you want to do is cruise at a nice pace, but you keep having to stop.

Every time you build up the momentum with a woman's bits, she is getting to the moment, she is enjoying what you are doing. Then you read the situation wrong and she runs into traffic and you have to start back in 1st gear.

It is as frustrating as it gets.

If you enter her vagina with your fingers make sure your nails are clipped. Nothing hurts more than a paper cut. Imagine one on the most sensitive part of your body.

If you are the type to stick your fingers up a woman's anus, then you might want to check that she is okay with that first. Some women might be okay with that. Whilst it may spoil the mood with others, and you could even face a sexual assault allegation.

Mud sticks, check first!

I know I stated in this chapter to be careful what you do and continue to reverberate this message throughout, but you also do not want to be too cautious so as to look like you do not know what you are doing.

Take control, anything you do decide to do, do it with purpose. Act like you know what you are doing and study her reaction. Stop acting like a pussy.

A lot of women like to receive oral sex, some women are not bothered either because they have never had it before or their experience of receiving it is nothing to brag about. Then one day she receives oral pleasure and her life changes.

Men know what stimulates their penises because it is their sexual organ, but a lot of the time men do not have a clue what excites a woman's genital area.

The problem with men is that they forget basic hygiene, and do not clean their teeth, tongue, lips etc. Any food that remains may affect her chemical balance. You are not a tramp, wash yourself!

Enthusiasm goes a long way with everything in life. If you are not really into it, you might be better off not doing it at all. Women are perceptive and she can probably tell if you are just doing something out of a sense of obligation. She will think that either you are rubbish at it or that you do not want to do it. Either way, this is just another problem with men, and she is not going to enjoy the experience.

If a woman uses her teeth on a man's dick it is likely to be unpleasant. Yes, there are some men that like it and there are ways that you can please a man's member with your teeth but that is a tricky technique to master. It is the same for a woman.

Do not bite her clitoris like an apple. She is likely to knee you in the face.

The same goes for her nipple but you might get a punch or a slap instead. Either that, or she could just terminate everything right there and then.

Be really gentle or do not do it at all.

But this is not the Karma Sutra, I am giving out friendly advice but if you want to be The Man in bed, do some research. There is so much information available to all nowadays, do not be dead in bed, take responsibility and improve yourself!

Then there is the actual love making itself. The moment every man on the planet cannot wait for. Take heed of the steps before as they are important, and without them sex may never occur. Often, these idiots tend to rush in and announce their lack of experience.

Do not be surprised if she complains to all her friends about it.

Do not bombard your way in when she is dry and when you have not discovered where the entrance is, then you are likely to hurt her and could possibly tear her.

Find a rhythm that you both seem to like. Try to make her cum before you do. Do not be a selfish cunt.

There is a lot more to it - but I am not your girlfriend. Let the woman guide you if you are unsure. Ask questions and remember the answers at the vital moments.

After the main act has ended, the problem with the horny-until-they-cum, thoughtless, inconsiderate, inattentive male species is that they will not think much about anything and just roll over and go into deep REM sleep. They start snoring like an elephant trumpeting, with drool trickling out of the side of their mouths.

A woman will lie there and may want to be cuddled, kissed, or even want her back rubbed or for you to do some of the things you did in the build up to sex like sucking on her nipples or squeezing her bum. She may even want to talk. Some might want to zone out and sleep too, depending on how deeply satisfying the experience was.

Minutes, hours, days may pass. The way you make a woman feel after sex will affect how she feels about having sex with you in the future. This is not constrained to those minutes or hours after sex. This may incorporate the days, weeks and sometimes months that follow.

If you cum, put your clothes on, and do not contact her for a reasonable amount of time then you might find your number blocked and deleted, your memory in her mind forever tarnished without a chance of reconciliation. That may not matter to you if you thought little of her and was not seeking a reunion, but if by some chance you wanted a favour, friendship, another encounter, or some form of entanglement – no chance!

Picture this: their eyes meet. The temperature in the room suddenly rises. She looks away sheepishly but not before sending a signal that she is interested. He floats over towards her with intent. His words slip off his tongue and sound like heaven to her ears. They flirt outrageously. They stare deep into each other's eyes.

They decide to take this moment of intrigue another step further. They end up passionately kissing, each rolling into one and another's arms on a bed in a dimly lit room.

Everything seems perfect. From the way he looks at her, his mesmerising way of talking, to his gentle touch and his lustful kiss. He presses all the right buttons and awakens her spirit inside and sends shivers up and down her spine.

Yet something is wrong. Something is horribly wrong.

She is ready for him to possess her body. She waits, anticipating with shameless desire within inside her.

Yet he is not hard. He cannot get it up.

Unwilling to accept defeat, she speaks softly and erotically into his ear whilst trying to stimulate every erogenous zone on his body she can think of (as she should do if she wants results), to no avail.

Disappointed, she does not know what to think or feel. She wonders if it is her fault or whether this is a regular occurrence. He apologises.

Some women will feel so disillusioned and hurt by this experience that they will lash out and call a man all sorts of names or make fun of him and destroy his poor little soul (that is what she should not do, but such is life). Whilst others will sympathise with his annoying dilemma even though this experience can be soul destroying for a woman. Others will just up and leave.

If he is super lucky, he may get another chance, but if he fails to perform on the next occasion she will be out like an investor on Dragon's Den (or Shark Tank if you are in the US).

What is it with these pathetic men that cannot get a hard on without the use of Viagra? And if you know you cannot get it up, why are you not using Viagra?

The sexiest woman could be put in front of them and they will show as much sexual prowess as Mr Burns from the Simpsons.

Another scenario: they are in the midst of it, passionately kissing, their hands are all over each over. He is penetrating her, and she is loving his rhythm and the places he is touching inside of her. Then he shrieks and starts to jerk like a car stalling. She was just beginning to enjoy herself but now it is all over. He rolls over and falls asleep. She lies there almost wanting to punch him in the face. This is another problem with men.

The one-minute man.

Men, can you do me a favour and imagine this the other way around. You are starting to enjoy the moment and build up momentum and then she pulls away from you and says she is done. You have yet to cum, but you seriously want to. It is not any different for women - they want to have their fun too. If you cannot last longer than 30 seconds do not be surprised when you end up in the rubbish bin.

Yes, sex is lovely and you cannot wait to penetrate her and have your fun but learn to hold off for a little bit. Look up tantric sex and learn some techniques to withhold that vital moment.

Talking about lasting longer:

Some men feel like a stud, their sexual techniques are good, and they last longer than a pornstar on Viagra. The problem with these men is that they take a little too long. She is exhausted and her private parts are becoming sore. It is worse if the sex is shit. She will be bored stiff wondering what to do with her life. You may wonder why she does not have sex with you that regularly. It is because she must psyche herself up for the occasion. She knows what is in store and she has to mentally prepare for it.

I cannot overstate how important it is to comprehend that every woman is different, and you need to read the signs and understand your woman. Some women will love a 2-hour session whereas others will prefer a 20-minute experience.

It is time for that all-important question, that every egotistical, insecure man wants to know the answer to, especially if he is not well endowed:

Does size matter?

The short answer is YES! It bloody well does!

Every woman I spoke to said yes. Only one said yes it does matter, but it depends what you are used to. If a woman is a virgin and sleeps with one guy then she may be totally delighted with her sex life as she does not know what she is missing, even if his penis is on the small side. She may never orgasm and be okay with that. She may have what many people class as boring sex in one sexual position. Again, this may be fine with her because it is all she has be subjected to and she is yet to experience anything different.

If your dick is smaller than her little finger, you might want to face up to reality. You are unlikely to please any woman with your pathetic excuse for a penis, even virgins. You better work on those cunnilingus skills!

If she talks to other women and they mention things (or she reads this book) which open up her eyes and imagination to different possibilities, she may become curious. She may want to experience what these other women or this book have been glamourising.

Even sleeping with a non-virgin, you may be having all the fun in the world and she might be wondering whether you have inserted yourself in her yet, whilst you are ready to cum.

That my friend is just not a good look!

A female friend of mine told me she had this exact problem with a guy. It was their first and last time. She just told him it is not going to work out without destroying his ego. He may have continued thinking that he is a master in the bedroom and maybe she did not like his personality. In reality, there are very few women that he will be able to please with his tiny excuse for a cock.

Denial is a powerful tool that keeps our minds sane in the worst situations.

If your dick is too short you may not be able to reach the places that make a difference in sex for a woman. There are certain spots that will make a woman jump out of her skin, if only you could reach them. If you have a long dick you are likely to touch those spots without even trying. She may also feel like your dick is going to go through her whole body and come out of her mouth. It is a pain and pleasure thing but not all women are going to be happy if your dick looks like your third leg.

The size and shape of the woman and the man both matters. I had this described to me in detail. If the tip of a man's penis is pointy, it is more likely to slip in easy, as the pointy tip has less circumference and eases its way in allowing the shaft to follow. Many women may feel like "Great; I will start looking for a pointy tipped dick boyfriend to have sex with". Do not start orgasming yet. A pointy tipped cock is likely to be more painful once deep penetration begins, as it is like a sharpened pencil digging inside of you. A more rounded tip may be harder to enter but less painful during deep penetration. It also depends how far their dicks can reach, if they are even trying to have deep penetrative sex, and so on and so forth.

If a man's girth is too thin, it may not even tickle the walls of the vagina and not build up enough friction for there to be any enjoyment for you. If his girth is too big it can be a really painful experience.

So, a man can definitely be too small, but you can also be too big! If you do happen to possess a donkey sized cock, do your best to arouse the women you sleep with, if you are not good at that, then you should use lubricant. Also do not just force your way in like a crowd stampeding to get away from a terror attack. If in doubt, use lubricant, as some women will need it, even if they are aroused.

Women are sensitive down below and you barging your way in may cause unpleasant friction or may cause her to tear and the whole session might be cancelled in a hot minute.

What a lot of men fail to realise is sexual enjoyment for a woman heavily depends on who she is having it with and how she feels about that person. If she has little feelings towards you, she may only enjoy the experience a little bit. If she worships the ground you walk on, then she is likely to have the time of her life (that is, if you are at least a little bit good in bed).

This also extends to her mood. If you just pissed her off or you are not her favourite person lately, even if she loves you, she may not fully take pleasure in the encounter.

That is why "make up sex" is so good. It is the same penis and vagina. But the emotions are high, you feel like you are lustfully falling in love with each other again. And the sex is mind blowing.

Some women may enjoy the act of sex as a stress reliever, but for others, low moods may equal a low libido. Do not be a dickhead, respect her mood changes. If having sex causes her to worry about things, like if she is having doubts about the man she is having sex with, or whether she might get pregnant, then sex might not be on the agenda for her until her doubts are relieved.

Get to know your woman, cheer her up. Find out the underlining reason(s) she is feeling the way she is and try to help her get back to her normal self, which might even be a new normal that you will have to get used to.

When people grow, they often shed their skin and become someone new. Be patient and grow with your partner. This could be happening over a long period of time but because you are not really in the moment with her or caring about whatever she is going through in life you are not growing with her. This is a way in which people grow apart and can become the beginning of the end. If you really care about this woman then get involved and grow together.

Read some books on how to be a supportive partner, watch some videos of the same ilk. The information is out there - you just have to look for it.

Do not become a smothering, suffocating person. Read her, if she wants space, then give her some. Offer your support but do not force your support or help upon her. She may become even more distant.

Seek professional support if need be. Get this right and you two could become even closer. Get it wrong and it could be the end.

You could do everything right, but she may not be ready for it all. Timing is key in life. You two may have missed the boat but if you are both committed to making things work and you are compatible, then it is likely to work.

Sometimes, shit does not work out.

Yes, this chapter is about sex and not about mental health, but that is the point, sex is usually more than just sex to a woman, even if it is 'just sex'. Us men are simple creatures. Women are full of flavour and are complex beings. What may seem straightforward to us may be multifaceted to them.

Another problem with men is some of them are just plain awful at sex. They might think they are God's gift to women when they are more of a curse.

They are either only in it for themselves or totally oblivious of whether a woman is having as much fun as they are.

The guys who are in it for themselves could not care less if a woman is enjoying the experience or not. As long as it feels good to them, that is all that matters. Be careful of this guy, he may treat everything like how he treats sex - with no consideration for anyone else, only his own selfish needs are important to him.

Then there is the dimwit who has little to no awareness or comprehension as to how a woman feels whilst he is banging away. He most probably thinks she is enjoying it and thinks he is king of the castle, but without any clear indication from the woman in question to this effect (you need to tell him the things that you like and dislike - whether he does them or not. If you are that bothered about him). He will continue in his blissful ignorance.

Men are stupid like that.

Some guys are considered terrible in bed by women - do you know why?

They are boring.

They do exactly the same thing every time, and they may not even do it well. Switch it up a little bit. She may like doggy style, but she might want to change positions every now and again. Try something different. Some men only have sex in one position. Some women are okay with this, others are bored stiff, waiting for this guy to hurry up and finish or catch a stroke of inspiration.

Other guys are a bit too creative. A woman is just getting into the swing of things and this guy changes it up as soon as she begins to enjoy herself. You keep killing the mood! She may not want to be in the same position all night, every night but she might not want to hang from the chandeliers either. Again, read the signs. If she is enjoying it, then let her enjoy it. She may be about to climax, but you just stopped and changed it up and killed her vibe.

Lovely.

Do any of you guys get the picture yet? Sex, making love - whatever you want to call it, is about being in tune with each other and intuitively moving in sync with each other. It is not a solo sport unless you are masturbating alone. Even if you are pleasing yourself with an audience it automatically becomes some sort of team sport, where the spectator is involved, even if they are not physically joining in.

Some women are fine with letting men take control and making all the decisions during sex, whereas other women have no problem controlling all the elements in the sexual encounters they have. But, if you are usually in control and she never gets a chance to express herself sexually, she may become frustrated. She might want to have a go sometimes. If she expresses this (this may also come in the way of a hint, be observant), then let her. You could be a control freak that likes to control every component of your life but for once let her hold the reigns.

It is not all about you.

If the opposite is true and she is usually the one to take control in the bedroom, then she just might want a break from the norm. Try reading her, she may not want you to change anything as she is totally happy with the status quo. But if she hints or says something that makes you think differently, then make the difference. Make sure you know what you are doing and that she is going to take pleasure in what you do, but at least do something.

Man up and dominate for once!

Women are not toys.

Trying to convince your sexual partner to put her legs behind her neck whilst having sex with you may sound great in your mind but she is unlikely to be that flexible. If she offers to do the splits on your dick then fine, roll with it, but if you are trying to create wine out of water it may be better sticking to government juice. When you bend and rotate her around like a game of twister, you might cause her damage. Be careful, you are both trying to have a good time, not to have a trip to the hospital.

Guys watch a lot of porn and they see these women sucking dick and explode at the thought of the same thing happening to them. They then see their girlfriends and push their heads towards their groin regions. They have seen it in porn, so it must work.

No, not always.

Some women will not mind this, others will be totally put off. You have to find this out before you start giving her a neckache with your heavy hand. Some women will not mind you telling them to suck your dick, but others will want to slap you in the face.

Even if she enjoys pleasing you orally, she might dislike being told what to do.

The problem with some guys, is that they have not learnt the art of how to speak to women. If she likes you talking aggressively to her then by all means do so. If she prefers the smoother, softer approach incorporate that into your speaking style.

Know your woman!

The requests from men can be astronomically mind boggling and disgusting to say the least. Most women do not want to choke up their dinner on your dick. Guys want women to do the most outrageous things. Not all men are into anal. The same goes for women, not all women are into it either. Do not assume that the woman you are being sexual with is into it. Even asking might get you blocked and deleted depending on how deep in her heart you are.

No, your girlfriend is not okay with you sleeping with her sister and is not willing to sleep with you while her female best friend or your male mate joins in. A lot of what you see in porn will stay there and never occur in your life unless you pay for it. I am not encouraging you to pay for it, I am merely stating to you that your fantasies are likely to stay in your mind because many women are just not interested in fulfilling them.

What sounds like a great idea to you, does not sound so great to them.

Condoms are sexually transmitted infections' and diseases' worst enemy - and many men's too. Condoms protect against most of the above and pregnancy also, it is one of the safest forms of contraception, yet a lot of men are just not interested in using them.

When women request that a man use one, the response from a lot of men is not dissimilar from if she had asked him to stab himself in the eye. It is not an unreasonable request, but many men seem to act as if it is.

The next time a man refuses - tell him you have chlamydia and watch his reaction.

Many men seem to act as if contraception is a women's responsibility. They act as if it has nothing to do with them. Most contraception for women consists of hormone altering drugs or invasive procedures of a doctor/nurse inserting something into a woman's private parts.

Countless men do not even want to discuss or consider contraception. They do not want to put a little bit of latex on their willies, they want a woman to do all the hard work whilst they have all the fun!

The best form of contraception a woman can choose is to not give him any. State this next time and see if he is still not interested in using a condom.

A woman may reluctantly agree to have unprotected sex, or she may get caught up in the moment and participate in the act. A man may or may not have convinced her by stating he will withdraw before he cums (which is not a documented way to protect from getting pregnant). In the moment, they both enjoy the experience, she cums (if she is lucky), he withdraws and cums, or he cums inside because he thinks he knows her monthly cycle or because he got too absorbed in the pleasurable excitement.

During the moment of ecstasy, she fully loved the moment, the second that he withdraws or cums inside her there is a feeling of dread and the realisation of what just occurred.

All for a short moment of fun.

He feels like the man.

She feels dead inside.

The effects of that sexual encounter can last until she has her next period. She will be holding her breath, full of anxiety until then, wondering if she is pregnant. Meanwhile a man will be getting on with his life without a care in the world.

Sound like a fair deal to you?

A woman will be looking forward to having her period, when usually she will be dreading it because of the pain, discomfort, hassle, and emotional turmoil it can bring. Every women's experience of their menstrual cycle may vary. Some women may endure all the elements listed above whilst others may experience less.

Remember, if a woman gets pregnant, it is her that has to go through the agony of an abortion, miscarriage or pregnancy and labour.

Bobby Black

What does a man have to do?

Nothing!

Yet a man wants to just slip in and slip out and leave a woman with all the burden.

No Means No!

Many women are friendly social beings. They are genuinely nice, welcoming people and think nothing of it. That is the normal state of affairs for them. Because a lot of men are useless at reading facial expressions or body language, any form of friendliness from the opposite sex seems like an invitation for them to assume what they like or do as they please.

Maybe some of these men were never treated in a friendly manner by females - or anybody in their childhood - so the first sign of friendliness seems like they have been asked out on a date, or that the woman is romantically interested in them.

When these women speak in a friendly tone, but the words are a gentle suggestion that they are not considering them in any sexual way, this seems to confuse these men's brains. Just to make it clear, you are in the friend zone and these women are not interested in you in the slightest way and they never will be.

Unfortunately, a lot of men fail to read the signals, even after a woman makes it clear and says no. These men still do not understand the language used and fail to comprehend why a woman's tone might get slightly aggressive, as her last resort to get her point across.

Most men will back off and get the gist, but you will still have some persistent, dumb male creatures still pursuing a woman to no avail, no matter what words or tone you use.

No means no!

It cannot get any clearer than that.

These men are stalkers, many women's living nightmare. They are like Max Candy in Cape Fear, clear fanatics with mental health conditions, such as obsessive-compulsive disorder mixed with narcissism, believing that any woman they desire will automatically desire them too.

There is a thin line between passion and determination versus barefaced stalking. Men can get so obsessed with women that they are borderline stalkers or actually become stalkers.

Now, I am all for men chasing women. Not running after them down the street - but romantically pursuing a woman, within reason. Many true love stories start out with the chase.

A man shows interest in a woman, maybe she plays hard to get, or maybe she is not interested at all. But eventually, with some gentle persuasion, the man wins her heart, and they fall madly, deeply in love with each other.

Sounds great does it not?

Fact is, it does not always go that way and some women just will never be interested in you, no matter how many flowers you buy them or how many cheesy jokes you tell them.

Imagine this scenario: a man sees a woman he likes and approaches her. She likes his approach and the attention, so they swap details. They begin to message and talk to each other over the phone.

Everything seems hunky-dory - at least until she starts to realise that this guy is flooding her phone with messages and missed calls. Like any normal human being she distances herself from him and lets him know that things are not going to develop any further between them.

Unlike a normal person, this guy does not take rejection too well and continues to inundate her phone with more messages and calls. So, she blocks and deletes him.

What happens next, you may ask?

This guy finds her online social media profiles and tricks her into conversing with him. She lets him know she is in a relationship. He then uses that information to guilt trip her. He talks about how she never gave him a chance etc.

She blocks and deletes again. Nothing too scary just yet.

Only now this guy has befriended her friends and he is turning up at events and parties that she frequents. She is now seeing him pop up everywhere she goes whereas she never used to see him at all.

This unfortunately is a true story, and it is one of many that happen to women on a daily basis.

A friend of mine was raped by her stalker. Sadly, we do not think she was his first victim.

It always seems to start off innocently. A guy being a friend or showing a romantic interest in a woman until they begin to realise one way or another, that the feelings are not reciprocated. This is when these dunce animals become obsessed with them and literally will not leave them alone.

I am unaware of the laws in other countries but the laws on stalking in the UK are pretty flimsy. Stalking in and of itself can be hard to prove, especially without electronic evidence. Law focuses on a crime being committed and evidence being built up to prove the guilt of the perpetrator. With stalking, evidence can be hard to gather.

When a woman is scared and her stalker knows where she lives it can be seriously nerve-racking, even after getting the police involved, because of the fear of ramifications from the culprit.

If a woman does get the police involved, the least she wants is an empathetic person dealing with the case. Not an untrained and inexperienced officer who knows little about victims or offenders of such behaviour. Often, women have said their experience with the police has left them feeling more like the offender themselves, rather than the person needing support.

That is, if they even deal with the same police officer. The first incident is reported to PC Shirley, but next week, it's being handled by PC Bob. Women then have to painstakingly relive their story to potentially unsympathetic officers.

Many women endure this fanatical behaviour, sometimes only for days or weeks, but others live through this experience for months or years.

The trauma this can bring to a woman can be devastating. The effects of having a man invade your life can last for years, sometimes a lifetime. Think about that the next time you are considering pestering a woman that is not receptive to your advances.

I am pretty sure some of these guys - if not all of them - have mental health issues and seriously need to seek some help. If not, some intervention needs to be taken by the authorities to help these wild beasts see reality for what it is.

No, she is not interested in you, nor will she ever be. Sort your mind out and sort your life out. Leave her alone. Go and watch some porn or do something else to fill your time with instead of preying on innocent women.

Rejection is a harsh part of life. We all face it at some point. Learn to deal with it.

It is not only stalking that this chapter is about. Many women go on dates with men and they go with the flow, after all, they are looking for some fun or a serious relationship. The problem with some men is that they cannot take no for an answer.

If you end up back at either yours or her house, this does not mean that she is going to have sex with you. She actually might want to have sex with you at a later date, but she is not ready now. She may be deciphering if she wants to have sex with you now. She may have even decided to have sex with you tonight but you either say or do something

The Problems With Men

that puts her off, or she changes her mind for whatever reason.

Women change their mind all the time, it is their prerogative.

At no time at all is it okay for you to abuse this woman and rape her. If you are kissing and your hand wanders somewhere on her body and she says no, guess what that means? No!

If she allows your hands to wander but then she notices you are removing items of her clothing that she does not want removed and she says no or stop; that means it is time for you to pull back and stop what you are doing. Do not force a woman to do things that she does not want to do. This includes constantly asking her to go further when she has already made it clear that she does not want to.

Too many women are subjected to sexual harassment and rape across the globe. Many keep it to themselves and never divulge the information to others because of fear of being judged or ridiculed. They live with the trauma in their minds and some of them never get over it. It can affect their encounters with men, even in innocent situations. They may feel uncomfortable around men in all situations. They might feel uncomfortable getting onto public transport.

They may find it difficult liaising with men at work or in social events.

It can affect their future relationships and their sex lives. It can change their libido and their desire to have sex, because they now associate sex with being violated sexually.

Be careful how you treat women. That could be your mum, your sister, or your daughter.

It was hard to write this chapter because I feel the pain of the suffering that these women go through when a guy decides that she now happens to be his pride and joy. Even though she wants nothing to do with him.

My friend that got raped is a close friend of mine. In fact, it is sad to say that I know several women that have been sexually harassed or raped.

Nobody deserves to be exposed to such degrading behaviour, that means nobody.

Mr Wrong

Have you ever noticed that most men always think they are right? You cannot tell them anything because they reckon they know it already. Even when these men are wrong, they are right. They will find ways to justify themselves so as not to look like the imbeciles that they are.

They can never just accept defeat in an argument or a debate just because their egos are too big to fail. They cannot handle that level of disappointment.

Most women, on the other hand, are more reflective. They are sensitive, but they are open to criticism. If you tell most women they are wrong, they may argue their case, but they will think about it and either in that moment or at a later date they will admit they are wrong or may have been wrong. If not to you, at least to themselves or amongst their friends or family.

A lot of men cannot live with being wrong or making mistakes. Especially admitting it to their female counterparts. Men cannot even admit it to themselves. They get into a mental state called cognitive dissonance where they literally convince themselves that the lie is the truth.

Defeat, being wrong, making a mistake or a bad decision is literally too hard to handle so they convince themselves otherwise and live in denial.

They cannot live with the fact that they are not perfect, they make mistakes or they can be wrong sometimes. Nobody is going to die if you admit a mistake. It is not a life-threatening admission.

If you know these guys are wrong, it is actually laughable. It is like hearing a young child caught in a lie trying to convince you that they are telling the truth, when it is clear as day that they are too dumb and inexperienced to know that the lie they are telling is too feeble to be believed by anyone. Whilst men try to lie their way through life, they are being laughed at because their lies are literally pitiful.

The worrying thing about it, is you will see it in world leaders in positions of power, who are mostly men, although the odd woman in power has suffered from the same egotistic facade. Rather than backtrack and admit that they may have misjudged something, got their facts wrong or have done the wrong thing, they will keep going full steam ahead, digging their hole deeper and deeper.

Just to save face.

A man will know he is wrong and bring that truth with him to his grave rather than man up and admit he is wrong or made a mistake. If a man does admit he is wrong, he will do so begrudgingly. He will mumble it under his breath so you can barely hear it. Or they will admit that they are wrong in one breath but tell you about sometime where you were wrong in the very next breath.

It is like when written news outlets broadcast a news story. It is front-page news (or front-webpage news) with the biggest headlines and the full story followed up inside in a two-page spread. When they highlight that the information broadcasted was a mistake, do you think you can find it? It is written in the smallest print on the most insignificant page, hidden at the bottom of the page or wherever you are least likely to look.

That is exactly how men are!

Meanwhile women have to live with these pathetic idiots.

The problem is there is nothing wrong with making mistakes, as long as they are not criminal or immoral, which can have long term ramifications for all involved. It is how we learn and progress as a human being.

You made a mistake, so what?

Nobody was born big unless you are Tom Hanks (in that movie he was not actually born big, but you get my point). We become better at the things we do by failing, reflecting on those mistakes, and adjusting what we do next time.

What Women Really Want

Submissive and neutral women are generally attracted to men that they perceive to be equal or superior to them in an area or areas of life that they value.

That area of life may be the physical form, where a woman believes a man is just as attractive or more attractive than her because of his handsomeness or his physique or both. It might be because of his dress sense which may add value to his attractiveness. It could be his financial status or his perceived financial status from her point of view. If she grew up in poverty and she still perceives herself to be impoverished, whether that actual perception is true or not, she may well find herself attracted to men who she perceives to be wealthy. The important thing is that it must be an area of life that she finds valuable in a partner.

Many women may be attracted to men who have a healthy bank balance, it also gives them a sense of security that this man should be able to look after her and any offspring they may bear. But not all women will value this area of life in a partner and many men may be confused as to why their immense wealth has little or no effect on some women. It is because she does not care, it is not important to her, regardless of her own financial status.

Another thing to remember is that positives and negatives are not equal. 1 plus 1 does not necessarily equal 2. One positive may equal 1 whereas another positive may equal 5 depending on what she values. The same goes for negatives. If a negative has a high value in her life but you have many positives, the one negative may outweigh all the positives that you have. You may be her ideal man but for the fact that you like to cheat. That fact is likely to negate all the positives that would have made you perfect for her in her eyes.

There is also another equation to factor in and that is that positives and negatives have different impacts and may last over a period of time. If your first date was a disaster do not expect to hear from her again. That negative will come too early in the process for any positives to hold any weight.

Positives and negatives can both have sudden impacts, but they also have another effect. Over time a positive or a negative can embed itself in the mind and/or heart of a woman. It must be noted that negatives tend to outweigh positives, as a general rule of thumb.

A woman may be in an abusive relationship for years. One, because the positive foundation laid down in the beginning had a long-lasting effect. Two, because the shock of the abuse may disorientate her for a reasonable length of time and cripple her senses. This may lead to her doubting herself and her worth, as in suddenly disbelieving her value to herself and others. It may also affect her judgement and ability to leave safely. Thirdly, the negatives have yet to embed themselves in her system.

One day when the positives finally wear off and the negatives have finally embedded themselves and she overcomes the fear of leaving (whether that be fear of him finding out before she leaves or wondering how she will survive if she leaves etc.), she will plan her escape route and up and leave. This is the reality of life!

Just because you may have the qualities that are equal to or are superior to a woman that you like, does not mean she does not value herself or that she will enjoy or even allow you to talk down to her or act dismissively towards her. Those may be the negatives that hold weight and put you out on your bum wondering why you can longer woo her.

Some women like arrogance and some mistake it for confidence and a man who thinks the world of himself above others may flourish with those said women. But not all women will be attracted to a man's narcissistic ways, there are many who are likely to be repulsed by this behaviour. Narcissists tend not to care what others think of them anyway, because they have already deluded themselves that everyone thinks highly of them. All who disagree have something wrong with their brains as to be so foolish as to think anything otherwise.

Just because you excel in many of the areas that she values does not mean she does not excel in many areas herself - and in many cases more areas than you. She has placed value on the areas that you happen to possess and that is why she has chosen you.

Over time our value system tends to develop, just like she no longer desires to play with dollies and you no longer eagerly and impatiently set up Scalextric like it is going out of fashion because you thought it was the best thing since sliced bread. The qualities you possessed when she first fell for you may no longer hold any value to her.

For example, you may have had a reasonable amount of wealth in her eyes when you met at a younger age. As time passed, she grew to realise:

One, that the amount of money you make is not worth what she thought it was. When you are really young £1 may seem like it is worth a lot, the value you gave it dissipates when you see how little it can buy.

Two, money is not as important as she thought in the beginning and other qualities have become more significant to her.

This may help explain why couples grow apart, for instance some younger women like older men, because they are tired of being viewed and feeling like a youngster and they long to be recognised and feel like a woman. They want to wear make-up, dress up in heels and live the life of an adult by doing the things they were restricted from doing as a child. An older man may represent this adulthood they are longing for. By being with someone older, they feel older and by being accepted by an older man, they feel like they are recognised by him as a woman, not a girl.

Younger women drawn to older men may lose that interest as they age themselves, because as she gets older the novelty of adulthood may wear off. In her younger years, men her own age may have been immature but as time passes men her age mature and are more on her wavelength.

The opposite could be said for an older woman seeking a younger man. They value youth and fear becoming old and unattractive. In western society, heavily influenced by the media, there is not much glamourisation of getting old, especially for a woman. Older women are not portrayed in the most positive light and are filtered out of mainstream media in favour of younger counterparts. In a younger man, a woman may feel vibrant and attractive to a demographic she felt she no longer appealed to. Plus, younger men are perceived as energetic in a sexual sense and that may also attract the older woman.

There are also men that are not the finished article yet. They are a diamond in the rough, but some women can see their potential and are attracted to that potential. So, you may show promise in the area or areas of life that she values in a man and that is enough for her for now. You may not even be close to equalling her in those regions, but you show enough promise for her to have faith in you. If you start to develop in that area or those areas, then she will likely stick by you. Even if you do not, she may still stick by you for a while but after hoping, dreaming, and wishing starts to fade away and reality starts to kick in she will dump you like a sack of hot potatoes.

Similar to men with potential, sometimes women are fooled when they meet someone new, either by the new guy or themselves.

When we meet somebody new, we tend to put our best foot forward and show the best of ourselves.

When we are looking for a job, we create a résumé to the best of our abilities, we fill out application forms highlighting the best of ourselves and we dress up in suits and shoes that show we are professional and take pride in our appearance. Then we try to answer questions thrown at us as articulately as possible hoping to prove we are the best candidate for the job.

When we meet someone we like, we act in the same way, highlighting our better points and trying to minimise or hide our negatives. This may give a slightly skewed picture of ourselves as the other person is only seeing our positive side. This may fool someone into thinking we are something that we are not, but first impressions tend to last until the truth exposes itself. How long that lasts, is as long as a piece of string.

Instead of bending the truth, sometimes people lie. There is not any reason to disbelieve somebody because why would we? I would like to believe that most people tell the truth. They might exaggerate a little or fail to reveal something that they want to keep private but, overall, I would think that people are pretty honest.

If somebody lies when they meet someone, that person is unlikely to question the lie as we tend to take people on face value. This can happen to a man or a woman and we can be fooled into believing someone is something different other than their true selves.

What women tend to do is think the relationship through in their heads in the beginning, before there is actually a relationship. They do not verbalise it to the man, but they are constantly picturing how they see the relationship developing or not. In doing so, sometimes they create an image of the man in their mind which is purely based on their own imagination.

They trick themselves into believing this guy is some fictional character that unfortunately for them does not exist, instead of seeing him for who he really is. Men can do this too, but I think women do it more.

I mentioned submissive and neutral women at the beginning because a dominant woman may be the total opposite. She is likely to be attracted to a man who is equal or inferior to her in areas of life that she values. She wants a man that she feels is less than her.

The point is women love men; they also love to hate them. They complain all day every day about them but there is a deep desire to be loved, desired, and wanted by the opposite sex.

Men are far from perfect, but we are here to diversify the world and enhance the lives of women just as they are here to enhance the lives of men (this may differ for the LGBTQ+ community).

Nobody is perfect. No relationship is perfect even if it might seem like it is to the outside world. The best you can do is try to find somebody who feels right to you and open up your heart. Allow yourself to love like you have never loved before, even if your heart has been broken before. How else is a relationship supposed to work unless you give it your all? If you do not feel comfortable doing that maybe you need to work on yourself so you can find the mental capacity and energy to make a relationship work.

We all just want to be accepted and loved for who we are. We want a relationship that works for us. Society, family, and friends like to dictate what we should and should not do but if you are in a relationship and it feels good to the participants within that relationship, then who cares what the world thinks? Why would you be in a relationship that the world thinks is perfect, but you feel uncomfortable in?

Do what feels right for you because you are the one that will have to experience it, not the world.

Author's Note

Now that you have read this book (hopefully you have enjoyed it) please leave a honest review on Amazon, it would be much appreciated.

Thank you

Bobby Black

The Problems With Men

Bobby Black

www.ingramcontent.com/pod-product-compliance
Lightning Source LLC
Chambersburg PA
CBHW022100160426
43198CB00008B/301